D1694699

#  Diplomat in a Changing World

# Diplomat in a Changing World

*by*

BERNARD BURROWS

The Memoir Club

© Bernard Burrows 2001

First published in 2001 by
The Memoir Club
Whitworth Hall
Spennymoor
County Durham

All rights reserved.
Unauthorised duplication
contravenes existing laws.

British Library Cataloguing in
Publication Data.
A catalogue record for this book
is available from the
British Library.

ISBN: 1 84104 029 0

Typeset by George Wishart & Associates, Whitley Bay.
Printed by Bookcraft (Bath) Ltd.

# Contents

| | | |
|---|---|---|
| List of Illustrations | | vii |
| *Chapter One* | Childhood and Before | 1 |
| *Chapter Two* | Schooling | 6 |
| *Chapter Three* | Early Days in the Foreign Office 1934-37 | 21 |
| *Chapter Four* | Egypt 1938-45 | 26 |
| *Chapter Five* | London 1945-50 | 50 |
| *Chapter Six* | Washington 1950-53 | 58 |
| *Chapter Seven* | The Gulf 1953-58 | 63 |
| | 1. Introduction | 63 |
| | 2. Bahrain | 72 |
| | 3. Buraimi | 81 |
| | 4. Oman | 90 |
| | 5. Conclusions | 97 |
| | 6. Postscript | 101 |
| *Chapter Eight* | Suez | 103 |
| *Chapter Nine* | Turkey 1958-62 | 115 |
| *Chapter Ten* | London 1962-66 | 150 |
| *Chapter Eleven* | NATO 1966-70 | 153 |
| *Chapter Twelve* | Retirement? | 163 |

# List of Illustrations

| | |
|---|---:|
| My Mother and I, c.1911 | 3 |
| With Great-Aunt Emily Gardiner, then aged 98, c.1913 | 4 |
| Speech Day at Eton, 1922 | 12 |
| The Lagonda being hoisted on the Channel Ferry, 1931 | 18 |
| The Egyptian Prime Minister and Charles Bateman, Chargé d'Affaires, 1938 | 33 |
| In the Egyptian desert, c.1939 | 35 |
| Wedding Day, June 1st, 1944 | 45 |
| Mother and child, Ines and Antonia, 1949 | 56 |
| New Year's Day reception at the Residency, c.1954 | 71 |
| Wind towers at Dubai, Trucial States | 86 |
| With the Ruler of Ajman, Trucial States | 87 |
| Hawking on the Trucial Coast | 95 |
| Mud-brick fort on the Batinah Coast, Muscat, c.1957 | 99 |
| Muscat, 1957 with The Rt. Hon. Julian Amery, the Sultan of Muscat and others | 100 |
| Turkey v. Scotland at the Stadium in Ankara | 120 |
| Greeting the Shah of Iran at Ankara Airport, 1961 | 143 |
| Princess Alexandria arriving at Istanbul Airport, c.1961 | 148 |
| CENTO meeting, 1961 | 154 |
| NATO meeting, c. 1969, with Michael Stewart, Foreign Secretary | 155 |
| NATO Nuclear Planning Group, breakfast on the Grand Canal, c.1969 | 161 |
| 'White tie and Decorations' | 164 |
| Handing out prizes at flower show, East Dean Horticultural Society, c. 1990 | 169 |
| Gardening at Durford Wood, 2000 | 172 |
| Ninetieth birthday party, July 3rd, 2000, with Antonia and Rupert | 175 |

CHAPTER 1

# Childhood and Before

WHERE DO MEMORIES BEGIN? Quite often we incorporate in memory things that we have been told. I certainly do not remember an occasion recorded in a photograph of me in a pram aged one, watching my great-aunt, who was born in 1815, planting an oak tree on the occasion of the coronation of King George V in 1911. She went on to live another ten years until she was 105, and she was able to remark truthfully on the outbreak of the First World War in 1914, when horror stories were being told about the German Kaiser, 'My dear, he reminds me of Napoleon'. My mother used to stay with her occasionally to give some time off to the devoted companion, known as Auntie Clara. On one such occasion she recounted that she offered to read to the old lady before she went to sleep and was asked to read something from the Bible. She started on one of the psalms and after she had read the first verse a booming voice from the depths of the four-poster replied with a correct rendering of the second verse and so on right through the psalm. My grandfather, who was this old lady's brother-in-law, had a curious career. He was in the Navy, rising to the rank of Commander, but got bored with the inactivity of Naval life in the second part of the nineteenth century and enrolled as an undergraduate at Oxford. He became a Fellow of All Souls and went on to become Professor of History. He was also a skilled genealogist and discovered that his wife was indirectly descended from a Gascon family (Brocas by name) who had come to England in the fourteenth century when Gascony was part of the English domains in France. They had an unfortunate propensity to be on the wrong side in various historical crises. They joined Edward II in his notoriously unsuccessful campaign against the Scots culminating in the Battle of Bannockburn, and one of them is reported in one of Shakespeare's plays as having been executed for his opposition to the successful claimant to the throne. On the other hand one of them is buried in Westminster Abbey, and they gave their name to a clump of trees on the river bank at Windsor, still known as the Brocas clump, in memory of the lands which they once held there when they had the position of Masters of the King's Buckhounds.

The Professor's eldest son, my father, was destined for the diplomatic service but fell ill at the crucial moment of the examination and became instead one of the earlier HM Inspectors of Schools. One of his other interests was co-operation with Cecil Sharp in the collection of folk music and dancing and he made a point of promoting this revival by encouraging the schools which he inspected to add these subjects to their curricula. My father was born in 1851 – 150 years ago. He married my mother *en secondes noces* in 1909. They had less than a year of married life when he sadly died before I was born in 1910. If this had been now, I would have been told that I had very little chance of normality, being born at a moment of acute tragedy in my mother's life and brought up an only child by a single parent. Fortunately at that time such terms had not been invented. It was a cruel blow of fate but those concerned had to get on with it, helped considerably by simple faith in religion, without apparently feeling that it was no part of the actions of a benevolent deity to create a scenario like this.

My mother's family was strongly Scottish. Her father, Alexander Macdonald of Lochinver on the coast of Sutherland, went, as so many younger sons of highland families did, to seek his fortune abroad, in his case in South Africa, which he seems to have done with considerable success. My mother was born there and they came back to England to enjoy a large country house in Sussex and a large yacht in which they sailed off the West Coast of Scotland. Alas, like many other highlanders, he then received bad advice and lost a large part of his money, so that they moved to a smaller house on the Black Isle in north-eastern Ross-shire. This led to my spending every summer holiday until about the age of 20 at a neighbouring house, where my godmother lived. There seems to have been no difficulty in going up there from Sussex even during the First World

*My Mother and I, c.1911.*

War, at which time I was taught to say grace after meals in the words: 'Thank God and the British Navy for my good dinner'. The surroundings were idyllic. Also, characteristically, the house was full of ghosts and legends, which may have had its effects later on. As a child I heard a noise as of a heavy object being dragged along a passage and down some steps in the upper floor. On recounting this at breakfast the next morning, the response was matter-of-fact: 'Oh, you heard that, did you?' From time to time my godmother's brother, on coming in to tea after his walk, would say, 'I saw them again today'. He was referring to the 'little people', whom he claimed to see disappearing under the trees. The most numinous place in the

*With Great-Aunt Emily Gardiner, then aged 98, c.1913.*

neighbourhood was a ravine thickly planted with trees, in which the Free Churches used to hold their services at a time when it was prohibited to hold them in churches. This was commemorated once a year by a service being held in this place, 'In the burn'. In the small and scattered parish in which we stayed there was the Presbyterian Church, the Free Church and the 'Wee Frees', all competing for custom. The Sabbath was still strictly kept. We were warned not to be seen even going for a walk on Sundays. Transport was still fairly primitive. A common way of going to Dingwall, the county town situated on the other side of the Cromarty Firth, was by rowing boat. The only disadvantage was that there was a large tidal movement in the Firth and if one got the timing wrong, the passage involved a longish walk through the mud before getting to the place where the rowing boat was waiting. My Scottish blood and my consequent right to wear the Macdonald tartan led to my taking an active part in Caledonian societies and in Highland dancing in various parts of the world.

Easter holidays included, from about the age of ten, an excursion to France or Italy. The first time my mother took me abroad was on a bicycle tour of Normandy in 1921, followed by a similar tour in Brittany the following year. Later destinations included Roquebrune, then a village tucked in between Monte Carlo and Menton, Portofino, the ultimate picturesque fishing village on the Italian Riviera a few miles east. Then a little later to Florence, perhaps my first exposure to European 'culture', where we stayed with friends of my mother's who were curators of the Museum in Casa Guidi, where the Brownings had lived. Another year we went to the Italian Lakes. My mother was an enthusiastic water-colourist and had long had the habit of going to where the scenery was best to practise her art. She described how once, some years before her marriage, she was sketching in a mountainous landscape in Corsica and after a time became conscious of someone standing behind her. She turned and saw a man festooned with cartridge belts, a rifle and dagger, watching her work with apparent interest. Not knowing whether she might be the object of banditry, she entered into conversation and after a time asked him why he was carrying all these weapons if not to rob the tourists. He replied simply, 'La Vendetta' – the family feud – without specifying whether he was preparing to act in self-defence or on the way to commit a murder.

This early travel may have been designed, perhaps half consciously, to familiarize me with foreign parts and so prepare the way for my assuming the career in diplomacy which had eluded my father. In those days young people were not asked so much as today what they wanted to do in life – and in any case the choices were not so wide – but the idea of a suitable future grew up in the family and was absorbed by some sort of osmosis. It might in my case have been the Church, since there were two bishops in the family, but this was never seriously entertained, perhaps because my mother used to recount that my father referred irreverently to clergy scurrying about in a cathedral city as black beetles. After visiting the Observatory at Oxford at a youthful age, I apparently declared that I wanted to be an astronomer. I cannot remember voicing any other aspiration.

CHAPTER 2

# Schooling

Schooling began with a year at a day school in Oxford run by two maiden ladies, during which time my mother and I stayed with her brother-in-law in the professor's house in Norham Gardens. We were quickly launched into Latin, in which you were expected to have a reasonably good grounding by the time you started preparatory school. From there to Summerfields, also at Oxford, a very conventional preparatory school with an uncanny reputation for gaining scholarships at Eton and other desirable public schools. Life there was austere and not particularly enjoyable. But then perhaps it was not meant to be. When my mother took me as a boy of eight to be interviewed by the Headmaster, his final remark after an otherwise satisfactory interview was: 'I hope he doesn't do music. We have no time for that sort of thing here'. That was the end of my previously promising musical career. I am grateful to this school for preparing me successfully to gain a scholarship at Eton, but one must wonder whether it was really necessary to have such a limited idea of what the education of a small boy should consist of.

When years later my wife and I visited the same school to see whether we would send our son there, I noticed, when we were being shown round, that there was a teddy bear on a bed in one of the dormitories and I concluded that things had somewhat changed since my time. We sent him there and he too duly got an Eton scholarship, but I am not sure that he enjoyed the preparatory school any more than I did.

Eton was much closer to the cliché description of school as 'the best years of one's life'. College, where the scholars lived, was a hothouse of classical learning, but with a good library where you could become acquainted with contemporary English writing and where the subversion of Aldous Huxley and Evelyn Waugh could begin to have its effect on young minds.

This may be the opportunity to reflect for a moment on the kind of education that was considered at that time to be the highest form of learning. We spent the years from about eight to eighteen concentrating mainly on the Greek and Latin languages during their classical periods, learning not only to translate the original authors but also to imitate their styles in writing prose and verse in the two languages. We then went on at University to add Greek and Roman history, again of the classical period, and philosophy beginning with the Greeks but extending to the present day. The justification was, I suppose, that these were the purest and most forceful examples of language, that a knowledge of them was essential to appreciate most later literature, and that practically all the political ideas which had been developed in later centuries found their origin in the histories of those two peoples. There was also the belief, held, though perhaps unconsciously, by many of the teachers, that by confining the teaching to the classical periods of these two languages, you were imposing a system which was finite. In other words the classical Greek and Latin literature which was available in our time, overlooking the vast chunks of it which had been lost on the way, was something which it was possible, with enough diligence, to encompass in its entirety. Therefore there was a right and a wrong way of expressing oneself in those languages, which made it easier to seek perfection and incidentally easier for the teaching staff to mark the results.

There are two main criticisms of this concentration on the classical Greek and Latin languages and history. One is that we spent an inordinate amount of time on the languages, to the exclusion of other subjects which might have improved our general education. The other is that by concentrating on the classical periods of the history of Greece and Rome, we were denied knowledge of the interesting and important periods which came before and after those times. For example we hardly touched on Alexander the Great because the historians who wrote about him didn't write such good Greek as Herodotus and Thucydides. We learnt little about the early Roman period pre-dating the Republic and equally little about the

Empire and its collapse into 'the dark ages', which has high relevance for the development of the subsequent nations of Europe. Our education could in fact hardly be called rounded.

There is another curious feature about the concentration on the Greek and Latin texts. Homosexuality was very severely frowned on at schools in those days and at most times was probably not widely prevalent even in single-sex boarding schools. But the literature which we were studying was rife with accounts of homosexuality as a natural part of human relationships, starting for example with Achilles and Patroclus and continuing through Sappho to Plato. (There is a curious ambiguity about the origin of the word 'platonic'. This is usually taken to refer to a relation of friendship which does not contain a sexual element. The *Oxford Etymological Dictionary* is blunter. It says that the word was coined in the fifteenth century 'to denote the kind of interest in young men with which Socrates was credited'). We were, I suppose, expected to make the rather subtle judgement that homosexual behaviour was all right for the Greeks and indeed was a concomitant of some great literature, but that it was definitely not permissible to us. Needless to say, no explanation of the distinction was ever given. At the age of about sixteen or seventeen I was a precocious classicist but rather unversed in the ways of the world. I was given some verses of Sappho to translate by my tutor (unfortunately only fragments of her writing have survived). After puzzling for a while at the text, I went to my tutor and said, 'But Sir, she has got the genders wrong'. So far as I remember he did not give a lucid explanation.

It has sometimes been said that the institution of fagging and the relations of the fag to the fag-master lent themselves to homosexuality. The system was that new boys at the school were, for a limited time, allotted as 'fags' to senior boys and carried out certain services for them like running errands and making tea. In return the fag master was supposed to be a source of help to the younger boy if required. It is quite possible that the system was in some cases abused, but certainly not in my experience or in what I heard at school. My fag master, who was the distinguished classical scholar Francis Crusoe, helped me in my early struggles with Homer.

It may seem strange that such innocence could exist. It was, after all, less than ten years since Alec Waugh had described the bad as well as the good aspects of public school life The literature which we were exposed to, much nearer our own time than the classics, continued to be ambiguous or to send signals which we were prohibited from following. Tennyson could write thousands of verses in memory of Arthur Hallam in terms which we would now think crept along a knife-edge of sexuality. But he became Poet Laureate. Rupert Brooke's 'rough male kiss of blankets' was not excised from his published verse, which we were told to admire. We were supposed, with remarkably little guidance, to know more or less by instinct that we should follow the Tennysonian definition of male friendship rather than that of Oscar Wilde some fifty years later.

Discipline was maintained largely by the older boys. The school was divided into houses, each with forty or fifty boys, and within each house a small group of the older boys were authorized to impose punishments for transgressions of the largely unwritten rules. These punishments included caning. How shocking this would be today! Only comparatively rare serious crimes were dealt with by the headmaster, whose sanctions also included corporal punishment.

One of the survivals of an earlier age was that the day started with an hour's school before breakfast, for which we were fortified only by a cup of coffee and a biscuit. It can well be imagined that productivity during this period on a cold winter morning was not high. Otherwise the food was copious and reasonably eatable. At that time each house provided its own food, in contrast to the central catering in force now. Drink was dealt with rather sensibly by a process of gradual inoculation, so to speak. There was a bar in the town at which, over a certain age, you were allowed to obtain cider. Beer was supplied in college to those taking part in the annual 'wall game', one of the two arcane forms of football which were practised in the school. Senior boys were from time to time invited to dinner by the headmaster or the provost, at which the usual complement of wines was served in moderation. These functions were, to some extent, intended as a test of one's powers of conversation. I was once invited with several others by the Provost when the guest of honour was a well-known cleric of the time who was known as 'the gloomy dean'. As well as being gloomy, he was also very deaf, and it was my unenviable fate to be placed next to him after dinner, when I had to struggle to make conversation by shouting into his ear, with the result that all the rest of the room could hear what I was saying. It did not make it any easier. During the more general conversation before dinner, there was some argument about the exact wording of the quotation, 'great is truth and shall prevail,' or whether it should be 'must prevail'. When this was repeated to the Dean, he said, 'No matter; neither is true'. It was a hard act to follow.

Although it is a few years out of order chronologically, this reminds me of another clerical putdown, this time at an Oxford high table. Father Ronald Knox, a well-known Roman Catholic priest of the time, was there prior to attending a debate at the Oxford Union. A friend said to him, 'I am surprised to hear that you are defending a motion that progress is inevitable'. Knox replied: 'I've no objection to saying that it is inevitable as long as I can also make clear that I disapprove!'

The Provost at Eton, who was a kind of Honorary Chairman of the Board of Governors, was in my time M.R. James, a well-known writer of ghost stories. His other great contribution to our life was to be in charge of the Shakespeare society, in which about a dozen of us met from time to time to read a play of Shakespeare for which he had allocated the parts in advance, himself usually taking the part of the third citizen or something like that.

A primitive element in our lives was the system of ablutions. We spent the first year in a set of cubicles. Each one was supplied with a small basin and a cold tap and a tin bath, also a large can with which one had to walk down two long corridors to reach a hot tap, bring it back, pour it into the bath, adding whatever cold water was necessary with a rubber tube from the tap. It can well be imagined what degree of bathing took place on a cold winter evening. Several years later when I was editing the school paper, I included a half-jokey item about the opening of the new shower rooms in college by a member of the Board of Governors. My report was frowned on by the authorities, who were presumably ashamed that showers had not been introduced before 1927. Maybe partly as a result of this primitive hygiene, I succumbed to an outbreak of scarlet fever during my first term at school, in the course of which I had to have a mastoid operation in the school sanatorium. It was performed by a brilliant surgeon who came down from London and all was well, but not before I had been prayed for in the school chapel. I was afterwards told that I was one of the few people who had survived this intervention. It was alleged afterwards that the sanatorium where my operation took place was not equipped with electric light and that the doctors had to rely on acetylene for lighting the operating table. I believe this to be untrue but it was symptomatic of the comparatively rudimentary facilities which then existed and which I am sure have been completely changed by now.

These comparative trivia are not intended to obscure how good and enjoyable Eton was, in spite of what now seems its excessive reverence for tradition. It was a living organism which demanded only that you took a large measure of responsibility for how you behaved and how you spent your time.

At about sixteen one took the School Certificate (which was later replaced by GCSEs etc). and then specialized in a comparatively small range of subjects. This is in itself a criticism and a contrast to the system in most continental countries, where the Bachot, which is required for entry into University, contains a much wider range of subjects. At this point I said that I would like to transfer from classics to science, but to no avail. I was rather ruthlessly pushed back into the classical stream, for two reasons, so far as I can guess. One was that my academic success in the classics might lead to the winning of scholarships which would credit the school. The second, entirely unexpressed, was, I think, the knowledge of the headmaster and others that science was taught at that time abominably badly and they must have thought it would be rather a waste of such talent as I had for me to spend the remaining two or three years of my school life in that field. No doubt things are very different now. I retaliated, so far as I was able, by playing an active part in the Junior Scientific Society, to whom I read a paper on the internal combustion engine. I made and

*Speech Day at Eton, 1922.*

installed a radio set and telephone in my room, of which the master in college was at first suspicious, not from any thought that these might be used for subversive purposes but because of the fire risk of having electric power available in a boy's room! The aerial for the radio set consisted of a length of wire insulated by two squash balls.

It is hard to conclude this section without some discussion of the place of the public schools in British life. Those who read autobiographies must be prepared to meet hobbyhorses on the way. But the question is one which, apart from questioning at home, puzzles many of our foreign friends, where the public school system (fee-paying private schools) does not exist, or not on anything like the scale which it does in the United Kingdom. Why are a fairly large proportion of the middle classes prepared to spend vast sums of money on providing a private education for their children which is liable to be interpreted as an example of exclusivity and class snobbery? Given this reputation, it is curious to recall that Eton was founded by King Henry VI to give education to seventy poor scholars. The others came in later because their parents thought they would get a better education there than elsewhere and were prepared to pay for it. These seventy poor scholars still exist in the form of the collegers, who, after getting a scholarship, can receive their education virtually free, depending on a means test. Obviously there is a strong social element in the desire of so many parents to send their children to a school like Eton. But there is also a strong element of belief that the education received there will be notably better than what they perceive in the state system. If the standard of education in the state schools in England was as high as in many of the French Lycées, the second element in the reason for choosing public schools in England would be absent. The French snobbery element, though of an intellectual rather than social character, comes later in the system, where it is notorious that entry into the Grandes Ecoles, from which the higher levels of French business and administration are drawn, is much easier for those coming from homes with an academic ambience than those without it. The element most to be criticized in the British educational system is not so much that those who can afford it send their children elsewhere, but that the state schools are not better. The abolition of the assisted places scheme, by which children from state schools could go, at virtually no cost, to public schools, was a narrowing of the base from which children can attain this excellence. It is almost surprising that the system of entering into a virtually free education there by means of scholarship was not abolished at the same time. The greater threat to the public school system may now arise from the positive discrimination against children coming from the public schools which is exercised or advocated in some of the Universities.

Fortunately this did not apply in my time and I won a scholarship from Eton to Trinity College, Oxford, and went there in 1929.

My time at Oxford was less than satisfactory for several reasons. We were so much encouraged at Eton to behave as adults that the degree of freedom experienced by some others on going to university was to us almost anti-climactic, and some of the undergraduate behaviour was not adult at all. Also I was sent to the wrong college as a result of attempted social engineering on the part of my uncle. His own son had been a great athlete and cricketer and, to compensate for these tendencies, he was sent to Balliol, which had the reputation of being the most intellectual college in the University. I, on the other hand, being academically successful and would-be intellectual, was sent to a college which prided itself on its success on the rugby field and the river, and where the atmosphere was not conducive to intellectual growth. This was only partially compensated by the fact that two of my tutors, Henry Price and Ronald Syme, were of quite outstanding calibre, the former going on to be Professor of Logic at New College, and the latter writing a seminal book on Roman Politics, *The Roman Revolution.* Moreover the timetable had been allowed to go wrong. I spent an extra year at Eton until I was already nineteen, in order that I should become 'Captain of the School', an honorific title given to the head boy in college. This meant that I could not spend the usual four years at Oxford and then take my first chance at the Foreign Office examination. The first part of the classical school there was 'Honour Moderations', which consisted mainly of the study of the Greek and Latin languages. This was usually allotted five terms. I had to do it in two terms in order to have the usual time for the second part, which consisted of ancient history and philosophy. The fact that I nevertheless got a First Class in Honour Mods was more a reflection on the inadequacy of that examination than of any particular prowess on my part. But the disadvantage from my point of view was that for those first two terms I had to keep my nose in my books instead of exploring the possibilities of other activities and acquaintances at the University. Also, perhaps, I was temporarily exhausted by the efforts to compress the examination process, and got a second class degree in the second part of the schools, known as 'Greats', instead of the first which I should have got.

At Oxford I divided my political sympathies with notable impartiality. I was a member of the Conservative Chatham Club and at the same time I subscribed to the Left Book Club, then being published by Gollancz. Although it is jumping ahead a year or two, it may be appropriate here to mention the much more violent political turmoil which was affecting some of my contemporaries. When I left Oxford, we were only two or three years short of the Spanish Civil War; Fascism was dominant in Italy and the Nazi movement beginning in Germany. The British and French Governments were being notably ineffective in dealing with, or preparing for, the gathering storm. Amazingly the Communists put across to some of the brightest people in the West that they were the only ones who could provide an effective defence against Fascism, somehow managing to gloss over the terrible things that were happening in the Soviet Union at the same time. Lewis Clive, who had been Captain of the Oppidans at the same time that I was Captain of the School at Eton, and Captain of the Boats, i.e. the leading oarsman of the school, who might have been expected to be a pillar of the establishment, went to join the Republican side in the Spanish Civil War and lost his life. A close friend at Eton, David Hedley, who went to Cambridge at the same time that I went to Oxford, joined the Communist party, went to America to preach Communism to the American workers, and died in rather mysterious circumstances there. I remember vividly one summer evening walking up and down the embankment in Chelsea trying to discover why he had to become a Communist and, ineffectively, to persuade him out of it. He finally said, as if to clinch the argument, that it was like falling in love. In other words it was a wilful abandonment of reason which made him prepared to forego his own independence of judgement and accept the decisions of other people as the leading principles of his life. I was not at that time acquainted with the three others, Burgess, Maclean and Philby, who under the same influence went further than this and finally betrayed their own country. They came briefly into my life at a later stage, which will be recounted. What is perhaps the most difficult to explain is their wilful blindness with regard to what was going on in the only place where Communists were in control of the government, namely in the Soviet Union. Evil stories about this could be dismissed as capitalist propaganda but as far as I know they never made much effort to discover for themselves the truth of what was happening. They were able on this point to give up the intellectual rigour with which their education should have provided them largely because of the depths of their disillusion with the Western democracies. The Depression was of course a contributing factor to this disillusion.

In the present age, in which someone has brilliantly remarked that the 'isms' have become 'wasms', it is quite hard to recollect how strong they were in the '30's. The awful stupidity of the First World War, the failure of the post-war promises, the attacks on middle-class values by such sceptical writers as Aldous Huxley, Evelyn Waugh and Orwell – all these factors combined to leave some bright young minds swept and garnished and waiting to be occupied by the new certainties. Nevertheless, I and the majority of my contemporaries did not succumb to these temptations. Those who did perhaps achieved greater notoriety than their numbers and influence really deserved.

An extra-curricular activity at Oxford which probably took up more time than it should was the driving and maintenance of fast cars and participation in some of the milder forms of automobile sport. This had started with a motor bicycle at school or rather in school holidays. The age at which you could, in those days, obtain a motorcycle licence was fourteen. I stayed with bikes for several years, including some quite lengthy tours through Europe and over the Alps. In the course of this time I took part in the 'London - Land's End Trial', which was an annual event starting in the middle of the night somewhere near Slough and ending at Land's End about noon the following day. It was not a race but a timed reliability trial, at which you checked in at various checkpoints on the way and then, in central Cornwall, climbed and descended various steep rocky hillsides left over from the tin-mining operations. One of the greatest problems was the inadequacy of headlights in those days. The lighting system on the ordinary bike was acetylene. This consisted of a cylinder filled with a chemical into which water dripped, controlled by a valve at the top coming from another cylinder of water attached to the lamp. The reaction of the water on the chemical produced an inflammable gas which burnt in front of a reflector and was supposed to illuminate the road ahead. This was a far cry from the halogen lights we are accustomed to today. I was lucky enough to win a gold medal in this trial. It must have been in about 1925 or '26. At Oxford I moved into cars, first sharing a friend's Lagonda, the make then consisting of rather basic sporting cars widely regarded as the poor man's Bentley. On one occasion we took it to a meet of Lagondas at Brooklands race track and drove it round the track in company with twenty or thirty others at speeds which, by today's standards, seem very moderate, but were too much for the basically tourist conformation of our car, which inevitably resulted in its running a big-end bearing. We clanked slowly back to Oxford and were lucky enough to have a friendly garage there which allowed us to use their pit to complete the laborious business of fitting new big-end bearings. On reaching the age of twenty-one, I came into control of a small trust fund which had been managed for me by trustees and I still remember the look of horror on the face of the elderly lawyer who had performed this task, not at all successfully as regards his choice of investments, when I told him that my first requirement was for £500 with which to buy a Lagonda. I proceeded nevertheless to acquire one on my own, which was the somewhat faster supercharged model. The university motoring club organized occasional tests up and down the muddy hills of the Chiltern forest tracks and on one occasion a so-called hill climb on a new piece of road that had just been built close to Oxford. The gradient was in fact almost derisory but the chairman of the club, when seeking permission from the Proctor (the university disciplinary authority) to conduct the meeting, took him for a ride along it and deliberately changed gear twice on the way to prove that it was, after all, a hill. Otherwise it would have seemed too much like a straight motor race, which was anathema to the authorities.

Another enjoyable activity was membership of the artillery section of the Officers Training Corps. This meant learning to manage, and ultimately fire, the British Army's then standard small artillery piece,

*The Lagonda being hoisted on the Channel Ferry, 1931.*

the eighteen pounder. These guns were still at that time regularly drawn by horses and not by mechanical means. So we had a lot of enjoyable horseback riding on Port Meadow just outside Oxford during term time and ten days or so camp in the summer on Salisbury Plain, where we met the real thing. Each gun was pulled by a team of six horses in pairs with a rider on one of each pair. One of the first things you were taught was that it is impossible to reverse a six horse team; therefore you had to be sure of getting the gun in the right place first time. Finally we lined the guns up on the crest of a hill and proceeded to fire live rounds at a target set up a mile or two away on the plain below us. On one occasion I caused some amusement and annoyance by landing a round squarely on the target and blowing it out of its emplacement, so that it was no longer visible for others to shoot at.

Perhaps a word has to be said about another leisure activity, or rather in most cases non-activity. There were four girls' colleges at Oxford but segregation between them and the men was still strict and there were few opportunities for mingling other than the annual summer balls. The majority of us, after all, had been to single-sex public schools and we were remarkably unaccustomed to dealing with girls, unless we had sisters of our own. And probably, if the truth be admitted, somewhat afraid of them? How times have changed!

On leaving Oxford I was lucky enough to win a Laming fellowship. These were the result of the generosity of a benefactor who wanted to encourage aspirants to the Foreign Service who might not have enough funds to obtain the language qualifications which were then necessary if they had not already done so at school or University. I spent the next two years in France, Austria and Italy having intensive tuition in those languages. The syllabus for the examination at that time included obligatory French and German to a rather high standard, also international history over the previous 200 years. I had added Italian to the two compulsory languages, because I had started learning it at school and on various visits to Italy. Austria was chosen rather than Germany because there was a particularly good teacher in Vienna, and perhaps because the growing Nazi movement in Germany might make life difficult there for a British student. This precaution almost turned out to be wrong because during my stay in Vienna in 1934, civil war broke out between the right-wing militia, the Heimwehr, and the Socialists, who then controlled the Vienna municipality and had built enormous tenement blocks for the workers, the most prominent of which was provocatively called the 'Karl Marx Hof'. Life in the rest of the city remained remarkably unaffected and everyone tried to continue with business as usual. The French Embassy, for example, held a reception at which they had invited the well-known boys choir, the Wiener Sänger Knaben, to sing. Halfway through the performance the lights went out and the trams in the square outside stopped running. Someone had blown up the power station or one of the electricity sub-stations. The music went on by candlelight until we dispersed through darkened streets. Although the Heimwehr were not strictly under Nazi influence, the fact of the deep division in Austrian society demonstrated by this little civil war undoubtedly contributed greatly to the takeover of Austria by Germany two or three years later without appreciable resistance.

By contrast, my stays in France and Italy were comparatively quiet. In order to be steeped as deeply as possible in the languages, we stayed in the houses or flats of impoverished middle-class families who found it useful to add to their income by being hosts to foreign language students. Two brief comments may give the flavour of what society in those areas was like in those years. My French host in Paris in 1933 was a retired army officer who had found no new employment since being demobilized after the First World War. He was in despair about the current political scene in France, to the point that he said on one occasion that he had 'La nostalgie de la guerre'. My Italian host in Florence demonstrated the rapport of the Italian upper middle classes with the artistic history of their country by discussing in art history terms any picture which I mentioned I had seen in my peregrinations round the museums. One could feel that not much had changed since the creation of these masterpieces a few hundred years before.

I narrowly failed in my first attempt to enter the Foreign Office but scraped in on the second attempt in 1934.

CHAPTER 3

# Early Days in the Foreign Office 1934-37

IN THOSE DAYS THERE WAS no training before taking up your appointment. You were assigned to a slightly older mentor who told you the mechanics of the business and then you gradually worked yourself in. Dress was a dark suit and it was customary to wear either a bowler hat or the soft black hat that became the hallmark of Anthony Eden. Security was practically non-existent. You carried no pass and after a time were recognized by the doorkeepers. If you had a car, you parked it without ceremony around the small green at the bottom of the Downing Street steps. Security in the more modern sense was only introduced some years later, as a result, so it was alleged, of a retired member of the Service describing how he liked to take walks in St James's Park. When he felt a call of nature, he would walk into the Foreign Office and when he had found what he wanted, walk out again. Another thing which may sound unbelievable today is that work did not start until eleven o'clock in the morning. Another legend had it that this was because it was useless coming in earlier because the mail coach had not arrived from Dover bearing the despatches from the Continental embassies. This gave time for riding in Richmond Park before a late breakfast. We had a longish lunch break, then later all assembled for tea in the Department and left as soon as we decently could after six. The most tiresome part of the programme was that we had to work on Saturday mornings, so that weekends were somewhat curtailed. I was assigned to the Northern Department, whose main interest was Russia. It also included Scandinavia, the Baltic States, which were then enjoying a comparatively brief period of independence, and Afghanistan. The last-named sounds anomalous but was a relic of the time when the main British interest relating to Afghanistan was whether or not the Russians were about to take control of it. I was never entrusted with the affairs of Russia, and so dealt with such subjects as the dispute with Norway over the fishery limits, the Whaling Convention, and minor concerns with the Baltic States and Afghanistan. Here the lead part was still played by the India Office since the then British Government of India had a far greater interest in what went on there than anyone in Whitehall.

There were two important principles for working in the Foreign Office and in the Government service generally in those days. One was that decisions were taken at the lowest level possible. That is to say that in-coming papers, telegrams, despatches, letters etc. were fed into the lowest levels first and commented on or acted on as they went up the hierarchy. Boxes of telegrams were also circulated to all levels, including the Secretary of State, as they came in. Occasionally a copy would come down to the lower reaches bearing his comments, which you were generally wise to take account of. Years later when I gave a lecture on the British administrative system to a college of government servants in Turkey and mentioned this point. I was greeted with blank disbelief. It seemed inconceivable to many of them, as it would have to many of our continental friends, that decisions were not automatically referred to the highest level so that they would be covered by ministerial responsibility. The other principle was that while a matter was under discussion, you were free to express opinions contrary to those expressed by others or even to accepted policy, but that once the decision was taken, at whatever level, you were then obliged to carry it out. The leaking mole was an almost unknown phenomenon. Officials had no business speaking to the press at all and leakage of documents to unauthorized people was contrary to the Official Secrets Act and therefore to an undertaking you had freely given. Now, unfortunately, it seems to be almost commonplace that if you disagree strongly enough with a policy you feel you have a duty to humanity or whatever to leak it to the Opposition or to a newspaper. This must be a great handicap to the orderly conduct of business.

My holding of the Afghan Desk led to one happy result. I was attached as one of the suite of the Afghan delegation to the Coronation of King George VI. This carried with it the privilege of being present in Westminster Abbey for the Coronation service, albeit behind a pillar. This was also one of the few occasions on which the diplomatic full dress was worn, including knee-breeches and silk stockings. The Afghans consisted of three uncles of the young king. They wore western dress but seemed to lope about the streets of London when moving from one engagement to another as if they were striding over the Hindu Kush. They were delightful people and gave me, in return for my services, a gold cigarette case which was subsequently stolen from my house by a burglar. *Sic transit gloria mundi!*

This period was also memorable for a certain *épanouissement* into wider spheres of life compared with the rather cloistered existence which I had led hitherto. There were debutante dances, visits to the ballet, where the last remains of the Ballet Russe of Monte Carlo were playing at Covent Garden. They were producing great performances of the symphonic ballets – *Présages*, *Choreartium*, *Paolo and Francesca*. How sad that these have been so seldom repeated. It was also the time when I began my intermittent devotion to deep sea sailing. A few of us got together and bought an old Whitstable oyster boat, which was rather roughly converted into a yacht in which six people could sleep. It carried an enormous gaff sail which required two people to raise it, and in very reliable weather a topsail roughly filling the space between the gaff and the mast. The effect of this was hardly worth the trouble of raising it, which more often than not ended in tears. Sailing was in some ways easier and in some ways more difficult than now. We had virtually no navigational aids other than the compass and protractors etc. of coastal navigation. On the other hand, the harbours round the south coast and east coast of England were easy of access and had moorings or spaces to anchor which did not require prior arrangement as they do now. Sailing used to take place at weekends and for a rather longer period during the summer holidays. We would go by train from London to wherever the boat had been left, sail for a day and a night to some other harbour on the south or east coast, leave the boat there, and return to London in time for work on Monday morning. One summer we went further afield and sailed down as far as Brixham in

Torbay. There the others had to leave and I was due to sail the boat back to some harbour nearer to London. I hired an ancient mariner from among the Brixham trawler fleet and we duly set off one morning in thick fog. We sailed on for most of the rest of the day, straining our eyes and holding a hand-held foghorn on which we tooted as loudly as we could whenever we heard the engines of a steamer. Luckily all was well and when we had got about opposite Eastbourne, the fog suddenly lifted and we were left with a scene of amazing clarity – such as I have never experienced before or since – due no doubt to the straining of our eyes during the fog, which had made them particularly sensitive when the light returned. We got into Newhaven just as dusk was falling and the next morning I packed off the A.M. to go back by train to his home, which was more of an adventure to him than sailing up the Channel in the fog.

We had another sailing adventure in 1936. One of the coronation festivities consisted of a naval review at Portsmouth. We decided to gather a few friends aboard our old sailing boat to watch this. All went very well until we started sailing up and down the lines of warships, when at a certain point we saw a very official looking steamer coming down in the opposite direction. It was not the Royal Yacht itself, but perhaps a pilot boat preparing the way for it. We decided it was not the moment to insist on the old rule of the sea that steam gives way to sail, and that we had better turn round and get out of the way. Unfortunately our boat was not very manoeuvrable in a light wind and as we were completing the turn, our bowsprit came into contact with the side of a cruiser. No harm was done except for a nasty scar on the cruiser's paint work. The Navy had evidently been briefed to be polite to amateur mariners and this was greeted by roars of laughter from the cruiser deck rather than the imprecations which we expected – and deserved.

Later in the evening the wind died altogether, so we had to rely on our antiquated engine to get us back into harbour. We had not quite got clear of the fleet when the oil level showed uncomfortably low. So what more natural than to stop beside a submarine moored at the end of the line and beg a can of engine oil, which was handed over with the utmost good will.

My next visit to a naval review some 30 years later was in rather different circumstances, as will be recounted in due course.

After two or three years the time came when I was due to be posted abroad. The system of appointments was at that time rather haphazard. The decisions or recommendations were made by the Assistant Private Secretary to the Secretary of State. There was no personnel department. The interviews relating to movements were carried out by him in the corridor outside the Secretary of State's room. I was told I was to go to Berlin. This was in 1937 and it sounded like quite an exciting post. However about three weeks before I was due to go, I was told plans had been changed and I was to go to Egypt instead. I flattered myself that this was because I had won the approval of the Under Secretary who supervised the Northern Department and also the Egyptian Department and wanted to keep me within his sphere of control. Con O'Neill was appointed to Berlin instead. A few months later he resigned from the service because he disagreed too strongly with the policy being pursued towards Hitler both by the Foreign Office and in particular by his Ambassador, Sir Neville Henderson – the famous policy of appeasement.

I often wondered if I would have done the same thing if I had been in Berlin. I was glad that I was not faced with the choice.

CHAPTER 4

# Egypt 1938-45

I ARRIVED IN EGYPT VERY EARLY in 1938 and stayed there until the end of the war in 1945. It was unusual to spend such a long time in one place but the war made travel to and from Egypt difficult unless one's journey was really necessary, and keeping the normal rotation of posts for a junior secretary did not fall into this category. Moreover I did not have any objection to staying there. I was promoted twice *sur place*, which was unusual, and personal circumstances argued strongly in favour of remaining. A great deal has been written about Cairo and the war in the Middle East, particularly good examples being Artemis Cooper: *Cairo 1941-1942*, *To War with Whitaker* by Hermione Ranfurly, and *A Cloud of Forgetting* by Pamela Cooper. I do not propose to compete with them and others who have written of the war. It may perhaps be more interesting to try to give a flavour of what Egypt was like before the war, and some descriptions of the land of Egypt and what life was like in the margin of the greater events taking place in the desert. There is another limitation. I was delighted to find myself in complete agreement with my publisher that these memoirs should not include the 'kiss and tell' stories which form a large part of many other reminiscences of the period. There was a good deal of kissing in Cairo and a certain amount of telling, though it is curious that the most blatant exposé of sexual life in high places was published shortly before 1938, that is to say well before the arrival of the 'licentious' soldiery, who might otherwise be regarded as primarily responsible for the looseness of sexual mores.

The British position was preponderant in Egypt at the time I was there and it is perhaps worth a brief enquiry as to why this was so. The French were the first Western power to play a major role in Egypt, when Napoleon landed there in 1798 with a large body of troops with whom he defeated the Egyptian and Turkish forces sent against him. It was at that time still a nominal part of the Ottoman (Turkish) empire, ruled by Viceroys appointed by the Sultan of Turkey. Napoleon's object was to block one of the main British routes to India and to do serious injury to British commerce. He had taken with him not only his troops but a large body of French savants, who made the first Western study of Egypt both as regards its antiquities and its present potential. This established a French cultural presence in Egypt which lasted for a very long time. One of those to take advantage of this French cultural presence was Champolion, the greatest French Egyptologist of the time, who used a tri-lingual inscription on a piece of masonry (the Rosetta stone) to decipher the ancient Egyptian writing of hieroglyphs. Napoleon's military success was, however, short-lived. Nelson destroyed his fleet in Abukir Bay and Sydney Smith resisted his efforts to capture Acre on the Palestine coast. Napoleon had to escape back to France in a single ship, leaving his army to be mopped up later.

After the French wars were over, the British and French vied with each other in lending large sums of money to the rulers of Egypt to promote industrial and agricultural investment. It was a Frenchman, De Lesseps, who brought to fruition the greatest of these developments in the form of the Suez Canal, at whose inauguration the French Empress Eugénie was present and one of the entertainments was the first performance of Verdi's opera *Aida*. Nevertheless, when a little later the Egyptian ruler (Khedive) got into financial difficulties and was about to sell his shares in the Suez Canal company, it was the British and not the French who acquired them. This was due to a brilliant coup by Disraeli, who reported to Queen Victoria, 'It is just settled; you have it, Madam. The French government has been out-generalled. They tried too much, offering loans at an usurious rate and with conditions...the Khedive in despair and disgust offered Your Majesty's government to purchase his shares outright'. The loan to finance the purchase was obtained from Rothschilds.

The acquisition of the Suez Canal made Egypt an even more vital part of the British strategic position worldwide. At the same time the money obtained by the Khedive for his shares did not bring about a lasting improvement in the Egyptian finances and the British and French found themselves obliged to set up an autonomous Caisse de la Dette intended to extract the interest on their loans from the Egyptian customs and other sources of revenue. A British official, the future Earl of Cromer, was made Controller General of the Egyptian finances in 1879. Immediately thereafter, however, there was a nationalist revolt by members of the Egyptian army against the government of the Khedive and a nationalist government was set up in 1881. This was too much for the British, who bombarded Alexandria and landed a force of troops which defeated the Egyptian army in 1882. The French had been invited to participate in the military action but refused and spent many years criticizing the British unilateral action and attempting to secure their removal from Egypt. Cromer became 'Agent and Consul General', and more or less took charge of the Egyptian administration. The apparently lowly title was intended to pay lip service to the notion that Egypt was still part of the Ottoman empire, and therefore could not have foreign ambassadors of its own. Cromer was succeeded by Lord Kitchener, who had reconquered the Sudan in the name of Egypt but largely with British troops. The Sudan was afterwards properly called 'the Anglo-Egyptian Sudan'. In the First World War, Turkey being on the wrong side, the ties between it and Egypt were severed and the senior British official in Egypt was given the title of High Commissioner. This symbolized more accurately the fact that Egypt was a kind of protectorate of Britain, controlled by the presence of large British forces and by British officials being strategically placed in positions of authority throughout the Egyptian administration. A fuller form of independence was obtained by Egypt in the 1936 treaty between Britain and Egypt, by which the Khedive was recognized as King and Britain obtained the agreement of Egypt that British forces should still be retained in Egypt for the purpose of protecting the Suez Canal. The leading British official became Ambassador instead of High Commissioner. This was the situation when I arrived. The preponderant political forces in Egypt were then represented by a triangle consisting of the British Embassy, the King, and Nahas Pasha, the leader of the largest popular party. The Egyptians had experienced many invaders and conquerors in their long history; the peoples from the sea in 1200 BC (whoever they were); the Persians; the Arabs; the Turks; the French and the British. The sub-stratum which went on, not necessarily so much affected by all these newcomers, was the remains of the ancient Egyptians, now represented by the Egyptian Christians known as the Copts (= Qypts = Egyptians). They lived largely in Upper Egypt but were to be found at all levels of society in Cairo, Alexandria and elsewhere. In the areas of their habitation they were still the traditional land owners and land workers. They had a constitutional position in the state which meant that in the days of democratic government there were always one or two Copts in the Cabinet. The physical type of the ancient Egyptians persisted among them and one could occasionally see uncanny likenesses to the great portraits and busts of the ancient Egyptians, even including the most beautiful of all, Nefertiti. It may seem surprising to class the Arabs as one of the invaders, but this was in fact the case. They invaded Egypt not long after the beginning of Islam and were able to conquer it the more easily because the Egyptians were having a quarrel with their Byzantine rulers over a ridiculous detail of the Christian dogma, and the Egyptians thought they might have an easier time under Moslems than as Christian heretics. Egypt is not an Arab state like the others in the Middle East. This is one of the many reasons why it has always been so difficult to make a union between them. It is also by far the oldest state among them, each invader having added some bits of his own but without upsetting the basic continuity.

What did the British add? Greatly improved finances, by which the state became more or less viable instead of in a constant state of increasing debt; irrigation and agricultural improvement; a high degree of public order thanks to a British controlled police force; a fairly brief excursion into parliamentary democracy, which, however, could not stand up against military dictatorship; a smattering of Western culture, due largely to the presence of a number of British teachers at the Cairo University and to the education in British Universities of a number of the senior figures in politics, business and the administration. One politician is said to have said to another, after a particularly blatant piece of skulduggery, 'I did not expect that of an Oxford man'. There used to be an annual Oxford and Cambridge dinner attended by a fair number of Egyptians. To illustrate the difficulty which many people had in understanding the political status of Egypt, at one of these the speaker was an English cleric who said, amongst other things, that Egypt was the brightest jewel in the diadem of the empire. The Egyptians present were polite enough not to correct him publicly. Egypt was never part of the British Empire. This was due partly to the curious interplay on the subject between the British political parties, and largely to the strenuous opposition of most of the other countries in Europe, particularly France, who resented the fact that their former control of Egypt had been transformed by the British invasion of 1882. It is a curious fact that the invasion of Egypt in that year was decided, after much hesitation, by Gladstone, the leader of the Liberal Party, who normally would have been classed as 'anti-Imperialist'. Salisbury, who became Prime Minister later in the decade, while criticizing the bombardment of Alexandria, accepted that Egypt was on the road to India and that much reform needed to be done in the Egyptian government, but nevertheless believed in an 'informal' empire and disapproved of any idea of 'moulding the Egyptians to our civilization'.

It was a form of indirect government which was turned into a doctrine in other parts of Africa. It was less comprehensive and pervasive than British rule in India, but on the whole it worked for quite a long time. It weathered the First World War successfully, even though the Turks had first penetrated to the far bank of the Canal before they were swept back by Allenby. There was some breakdown in security immediately after the First War but this did not last. The system demanded a certain amount of make-believe on all sides but in an area in which the Thousand and One Nights was an important part of the literary heritage, this perhaps was not too difficult. In the Second World War the Egyptians accepted without difficulty that we should fight our battles from and on their territory without asking them to take part. They may not have liked us very much, but they were wise enough to realise that they would have a worse time under the Germans. The triangle of forces mentioned above, the King, the British, the Nationalist Popular Party (Wafd), was put to its severest test in 1942. Our fortunes were at a low ebb with the Germans advancing towards Alexandria. It was believed that the Government installed by King Farouk was at least not whole-hearted in its support of the Allied cause and that there were some elements that might be preparing for a German entry into the populated parts of Egypt. The Ambassador (Lord Killearn), was authorized to demand that either the King should abdicate, leaving the throne to an elderly relative who was reputedly more enthusiastic about the Allied cause, or should immediately appoint Nahas Pasha, leader of the Wafd party, as his Prime Minister. Killearn went to carry out this mission accompanied by a British Army tank which broke down the gates of the palace, whereupon he had his interview with King Farouk, who accepted the alternative of appointing Nahas. Apart from this one incident, there was no internal security problem in Egypt during the war and no British troops had to be deployed to deal with it. This was a remarkable tribute to the validity of the system which had been developed there.

Although it relates to a period after I had left Egypt, one must put the question why, if it had been so successful up to then, the system finally broke down. The simple answer is that we stayed too long and misjudged the strength of nationalist opinion. Our evacuation of India in '47-'48 was a precedent which other peoples could feel might be applied in their case as well. The creation of the state of Israel, and the poor showing of the Egyptian army in the war that inevitably followed this event, which the army blamed on the politicians and on the king for not having equipped them better, prepared the way for the military coup against the government and the King in 1952. This was followed by the withdrawal of British troops from their previous positions in Cairo and Alexandria to the Canal zone, from which in turn they were driven by revolt and guerrilla actions two years later.

I can claim a small amount of credit for having foreseen some of these problems and proposed a plan which might possibly have avoided some of them. While the war was still going on, I suggested that after it was finished the British forces should move to the other side of the Suez Canal and create a base in Sinai, the peninsula which belongs to Egypt but is separated from the inhabited parts of the country by the Canal. I had travelled a good deal in Sinai and suggested it might form an ideal place to station troops, since there were virtually no local inhabitants and you could command the Canal equally well from the far bank as by the existing arrangements. The proposal was turned down by my superiors on the grounds that it was unnecessary. We would always be able to maintain large forces in Egypt and there was no need to go to the expense and trouble of moving them to the other side of the Canal.

To complete this part of the picture, I think I am bound to try to give an opinion on the forcible action taken to make the King change his government and to comment on the character of the King himself, with whom I was privileged to have some acquaintance. As things stood in 1942, I think it was a risk that we could not afford to take that there should be a weakening in the home front in Egypt at a time when the British forces were being hard pressed about seventy or eighty miles away. Therefore it was right in the circumstances at that time to bring about a change of government which would avoid this danger. As to the methods used, it is a good principle, on the very rare occasions on which it is permissible for a diplomat to intervene in the affairs of his host country, that one should get one's man in. In such circumstances it is no good approaching the matter half-heartedly. The problem for us came later when, having exercised this preponderant power during the war on the whole successfully, we failed to recognise that a new situation existed which had to be dealt with by very different methods.

Farouk was unlucky in coming to the throne so young and with such inadequate preparation and then in being faced with a succession of events of quite exceptional difficulty and without advisers of a character to match the extremity of the times. My wife and I became acquainted with King Farouk through our great friends in the American Embassy, John and Josie Brinton. He used to come from time to time, unannounced, to the Thursday evening parties

*The Egyptian Prime Minister and Charles Bateman, Chargé d'Affaires, 1938.*

that we had in our flat overlooking the Nile, where he could meet people from all areas of Cairo's society: British officers just returned from some hazardous mission to Greece or Yugoslavia, writers and poets who found a second home in Egypt after having had forcibly to leave Greece, British and American journalists, and of course some pretty girls. He had a reputation for womanizing, but on these occasions he behaved with perfect propriety, and never touched a drop of alcohol. On another occasion he invited the Brintons and ourselves to go with him to his country house in the Delta to spend the afternoon. We joined his car at the palace in Cairo, and he casually tossed a revolver into the front seat next to him and set off with no other protection, to drive fifty miles into the countryside to a beautiful house and garden where we had a swim and he gave us tea and recited nursery rhymes that he had learned from his English governess. Once he dropped in, also unannounced, at the country house where we used to stay during the summer just outside Cairo and spent the night with two of his hangers on (male). There was never any evidence why he did this. I strongly suspect that he had some, as it turned out false, information that an attempt might be made on him if he stayed in his usual haunts. Everything in fact passed off peacefully and he left after breakfast the next morning. Farouk had had a very difficult childhood. His mother, by all accounts, was in no position to give him a serious moral upbringing. His father paid little attention and his early years, after the English governess, were spent in the company of the palace servants. He then went briefly to Woolwich (The Royal Artillery College outside London), and had an English tutor for a short while. His father then died and Farouk ascended the throne aged seventeen, the other two players in the 'triangle', the British Ambassador and Nahas, being about three times that age.

It was not easy to have any serious conversation with him but I recall one memorable remark. I had asked him how he saw the future of the Suez Canal after the end of the war. He answered without a moment's hesitation that the best thing would be to fill it in. If one reflects on the history of the Canal and of foreign interest in it, it is not difficult to see that it was of no very great value to Egypt except for the fees which ships paid for passing through, which until 1956 went largely to the French-owned Suez Canal Company. If it had not existed, there might have been much less foreign intervention in the affairs of Egypt. It was a paradoxical view, but one that deserved to be taken quite seriously.

One of the many joys of living in Egypt, especially before the outbreak of the war, was the facilities for enterprising travel. The destinations were largely archaeological. Obviously one could not live long in Egypt without becoming an amateur Egyptologist. There were not only the great pyramids of Giza but also the earlier ones at Saqqara, and there were also fascinating remains of the Greeks and Romans, and the whole medieval world of the Cairo mosques. The desert was an invitation in itself, the maps still crossed by dotted lines with the names of the first person who had done that particular traverse and the date. The patron saint of desert travel was Bagnold, who had left Egypt by the time I got there but left as his legacy the book *Libyan Sands*, describing not only the far-away places he had

*In the Egyptian desert, c.1939.*

visited but the techniques of desert travel by car The trouble about desert tracks was that they got covered by blown sand, so that you sometimes had to go by compass bearing, but compasses do not work well in cars, so Bagnold invented the sun compass, a kind of glorified sun dial which was mounted on the front wing of the car and you drove according to the shadow of the gnomon. I constructed one of these for our major excursion in the Western desert and we relied on it successfully. Four-wheel drive had hardly been invented and was certainly not commonly available, so we travelled in old Fords with oversized tyres and carried rope ladders which helped to give the wheels a grip when climbing sand dunes.

One of the favourite destinations was the Greek monastery of Sinai, situated high up in the mountains of that peninsula and reputedly the site where Moses received the Ten Commandments from the Deity. The monastery was built by the Byzantine Emperor Justinian in the sixth century and had been inhabited ever since by Greek Orthodox monks. It was to some extent fortified but the inhabitants usually managed to remain on good terms with the neighbouring Arab tribesmen. The monastery was reached by crossing the Suez Canal at Suez and after a stony road along the shore, turning inland up a rough and sandy track for another few hours. The monks would offer accommodation and hospitality but we usually preferred to camp outside. The desert scenery on the way was breathtaking in its range of pastel colours. The monastery had a collection of pictures of Byzantine Emperors and church dignitaries. We were shown round once by one of the monks, who stopped in front of one of the Emperors' portraits and said, 'This was a great Christian. He killed many heathen.' It also contained a library of repute, which had however been plundered by various travellers during the ages. One of these – I think a Russian traveller of the last century – had purloined a priceless manuscript of the bible known as the Codex Sinaiticus. Later this had come into the possession of the British Museum, who in the 1930's had the bright idea, not of returning it to the library in Sinai, but of sending them a facsimile copy which had been made in England. I was present in the Embassy when the Ambassador presented this copy to the Patriarch of the monastery. I must say, it was an embarrassing occasion.

There were several places of great interest down the east coast of Egypt and in the one or two valleys which joined it to the Nile. There were ancient Greek monasteries which were believed to be places where monasticism had originated in the early centuries of Christendom, some still inhabited by a few monks. Further down, about half way across between the Red Sea and the Nile, there was a granite quarry used by the Romans They had extracted from it some of the columns which later adorned Rome. There was still lying there a column which had broken before they could get it out and countless chisel marks showing how they had cut into the granite bedrock. The columns were apparently transported to the Nile on rollers and then floated to the sea and across the sea to Rome. Further down and nearly on the coast, there was one of the very few porphyry mines in existence, from which the Byzantines had derived the columns and facings which they so prized. The track leading into the now deserted quarry was carpeted with red dust. The Byzantine

Emperors who succeeded their fathers or other senior members of their family were described as Porphyrogenitus – born in the purple – but I think this referred more to the fabrics dyed with the purple dye obtained from certain molluscs found in the Eastern Mediterranean, to which the same Greek word for purple was applied. There is another curious historical trail relating to this colour which I put forward without adequate evidence. The Byzantine Emperors signed their laws or decrees or correspondence in purple or red ink. In the Foreign Office in my time the privilege of signing in red ink was reserved in London to the Foreign Secretary, abroad to Ambassadors. It would be nice to think that this usage, which by now has probably disappeared as being too old fashioned or politically incorrect, represented a claim to be in the succession of the Emperors.

There was one more *objet de voyage* on the Red Sea coast, right down at almost the extreme south-eastern corner of Egypt. In the hills near the coast there was a very small goldmine operated, very improbably, by a white Russian whose family had been stranded in Egypt after the Russian Revolution, and his glamorous wife from Cairo. We visited them, driving endlessly down the corrugated road along the Red Sea coast and finally turning up into the hills and passing a very agreeable two or three days in what must have been one of the loneliest places on earth.

But for serious desert travel one went to the Western desert. Eighteen months or so before the outbreak of war this was still almost entirely empty and contained several sites of great interest to the intrepid traveller. There was, for example, the Siwa oasis, which Alexander the Great had visited during his brief time in Egypt to consult the oracle of the God Amun. When I went there it was still probably more or less the same as when he had visited it some 2,300 years before. There was a remarkable outpouring of fresh water with date plantations and a few ancient buildings. Further south there was a semi-circle of four oases, each one with fresh water in varying quantities, which allowed the cultivating of date palms. The first was Bahariya, a long but not too difficult stony trek from Cairo. From there to the almost unknown Farafra, a tiny settlement which seemed almost on the edge of extinction, reached by very difficult sand, in which every now and then one fell into a pocket of gypsum with clouds of white dust rising up and penetrating everywhere. This was where we had to have successful recourse to the sun compass. Then on to the two much larger and more prosperous oases further south, Dakhla and Kharga. These had quite large populations, where we were received in a very friendly manner and given to eat the part of the palm tree extracted from the growing point and leading inevitably to the death of the tree – so it was a munificent addition to the menu. At Dakhla there was a stone tablet with a long textual inscription confirming the fact that the Roman Empire had extended to this point and giving rise to wonder at the fortitude of the Romans in travelling long waterless stretches either on foot or perhaps by camel, though I am unaware of any reference to a Roman camel corps.

From Kharga the course was back to the Nile Valley, but first one had to get up on to a stony plateau by negotiating a steep, sandy gully where the rope ladders came into full play to allow the cars to plough their way to the top. Finally down to the valley, where we found ourselves almost opposite Luxor, site of the most famous archaeological tombs from the times of the Pharaohs. We stayed a short time there in great comfort after our desert travel, and saw what we could of the antiquities. Then we set off back to Cairo by the Nile valley road, which offered no particular difficulties except for the extraordinary clouds of dust which forced us to travel about a mile apart. We stayed the night with Coptic friends in Upper Egypt and then made our way successfully back to Cairo.

In the early part of 1939 I was tempted by the ultimate goal of desert travel, the tiny oasis of Uweinat in the far south-west of Egyptian territory, where it joined with Libya and the Sudan. This had been accomplished with great aplomb on camel back by Hassanein Pasha, an official of the Egyptian court, and Rosita Forbes, an English lady journalist, a few years before. It had also been reached by the great Bagnold already referred to. This and the mountain range immediately to the north, Gilf al Kabir, featured largely in the book and film, *The English Patient*. The exploration aspects of this story were to a large extent factual, apart from the embellishment of the love affair and the eventual fate of the Hungarian explorer Almasy. He was a real person who, after taking part with British officers in this exploration, went over to the Germans at the beginning of the war and successfully guided a German spy across the desert into the Nile valley. The spy was picked up in Cairo not long afterwards but Almasy never reappeared there so far as is known.

The prospects of this journey were quite hazardous. Owing to the very long distances, it was necessary to establish a dump of petrol far out in the desert that we could use on the way back. The cars that we had available were simply not big enough to carry enough petrol for the whole journey out and back. This was more or less standard procedure for journeys of this kind at this time, but it depended on the chance that the local Bedouin inhabitants would not use the dump for target practice meanwhile. Equally tricky was the fact that the boundaries in the neighbourhood of Uweinat were not at all well defined on the ground and we would have to tell the Italians before we went in case we strayed into their territory by mistake. They had received Bagnold very hospitably when he arrived there a few years before, but now the relations between our two countries were balanced on a knife edge and nothing could be taken for granted. Before any of this, the first step was to clear the journey with the Egyptian authorities and I went to call on a British officer who was in command of the camel corps, which patrolled the Western desert in a sketchy manner. After I had described my plans, he asked me who was going with me, I said my chief companion would be Vladimir Peniakoff, a white Russian who had lived in Egypt all his life and was manager of a Belgian sugar factory and a most experienced desert traveller. The reply rather took me aback. 'Oh dear, we don't want any foreigners in that area do we?' The remark turned out to be exceptionally ironical. Peniakoff later commanded an irregular formation loosely attached to the British Army in the western desert and operating often behind enemy lines, known as Popski's private army and performing feats of extraordinary bravery. Peniakoff later recorded his exploits in his book, *Popski's Private Army* (published by Jonathan Cape in 1950 and republished by the Re-Print Society in 1953). He refers in that book to the preparations for the planned journey to Uweinat, which never took place, and says that he used his memory of the geography which he had acquired at that time to extricate himself when he was temporarily lost near the Gilf Al Kabir. Even without the benefit of this hindsight, the obstacles could probably have been overcome in early 1939, but the approach of war finally made any plans of this kind unrealistic.

But travel in other directions was not altogether brought to an end. There was one memorable trip to Petra in 1941, but on the whole we had to concentrate on more serious business. In the early months of the war, after the fall of France, Cairo had an extraordinary position as the second centre of war effort after London and virtually the only place in which land battles involving British troops were planned and executed. It was also a centre for sideshows of varying importance. Early on there was a fortunately abortive plan to raid the oil fields in Rumania, which involved our spending a morning stuffing naval uniforms into diplomatic bags for transport to Bucharest. Rumania was at that stage still nominally neutral and the idea was that a party of naval personnel should arrive there in civilian clothes (I am not sure whether described as tourists or what else) and then put on their naval uniforms and travel up the Danube by boat until they reached the oilfields, which they would proceed to sabotage. The uniforms were necessary because if they had carried out the operation in civilian clothes, they would have been liable to have been shot as spies. Fortunately the operation was called off before it was put into practice.

A much more serious 'sideshow' was the Abyssinian campaign to turn the Italians out of Ethiopia. My first brush with this operation was a curious example of the rather odd bits of support which the Embassy was called upon from time to time to offer the military. While we were still in Alexandria (where the Embassy went for the summer months) in the summer of 1939, and dispositions were already being taken with a view to the warlike operations that were likely to follow shortly, we received orders to take over a large consignment of 'Maria Theresa dollars' which were arriving in

Alexandria by cruiser and had to be delivered to Khartum, the capital of the Sudan. This currency had a curious history, with not all of which I am familiar. The coins were minted in Vienna in the 18th century with a fine portrait of the empress on one side. By some curious quirk of commerce, they became the preferred currency of large parts of Arabia and East Africa and were still in this position in 1939. The mint in Austria had, I think, already ceased making these coins and replicas were therefore made by the Royal Mint in England. The coins were going to be needed to pay the expenses of the foreseeable campaign against the Italians in Abyssinia. (My second acquaintance with this currency came several years later when I was in the Persian Gulf and these coins were still current in Southern Arabia, so that when I went to visit the Sultan of Muscat in his southern capital of Salalali, they were the only currency that was readily acceptable. I used to set out carrying a bag of them with which to tip the servants etc.)

Reverting to Alexandria in 1939, I was fortunate enough to have a friend in the Army Transport Service who was willing to provide a six-ton lorry and a small escort to receive the consignment from the cruiser in Alexandria harbour and transport it to the railway station, where we hoped to find military personnel who would escort it by train to Khartum. It only remained to brief confidentially the Assistant Commander of the police in Alexandria, who was still a British officer, to make sure that we could have free passage in and out of the harbour. In the event all went well. We drove alongside the ship and received I do not know how many heavy boxes of these silver coins, loaded them into the six-tonner and drove off to the station. There we found a train shortly due to depart carrying a unit of British forces southwards and persuaded a rather reluctant officer to take charge of the boxes for delivery to his destination at the British Forces headquarters in Khartum. The Ambassador reported this unusual transaction to London, adding that it had been rather awkward receiving such short notice, to which he received a reply congratulating us on its success and saying that they had been confident that the Embassy would find a way of meeting the emergency.

A little later on, when the Abyssinian campaign was in progress, Orde Wingate passed through Cairo on his way to take command of the guerrilla operation which succeeded in restoring the Emperor, Haile Selassie, to his throne. It was impossible not to be impressed by Wingate's enthusiasm and idealism. Another person who was deeply involved in that campaign under Wingate was Wilfred Thesiger, who had been my contemporary at school and whose traces I subsequently found in Arabia, where he had made some startling journeys across the desert of the 'empty quarter'. His account of Wingate is vivid and not always entirely complimentary. Wingate was clearly one of that breed of great eccentrics whom the war threw up and who, by his own very individualistic methods, made a great contribution.

But the dark days of 1942, when the German forces had reached only about sixty miles from Alexandria and the British Forces occupied the Alamein line, concentrated our attention nearer home. While the outcome of the forthcoming battle was still uncertain, we had to take one or two drastic precautionary measures. First there was 'Ash Wednesday', when we at the Embassy had to destroy all our archives. We did this in great braziers which were set up in the courtyard of the office and it was said that fragments of vital papers descended on the rest of Cairo for the next day or two. Then I had the very painful task of warning the representatives of governments under German occupation, such as the Dutch and the Belgians, that in our view they ought to prepare to get out of Egypt before the Germans arrived, since they would be particularly at risk representing governments that had moved outside their countries rather than submit to German occupation.

We had at that time the practice that one of us would sleep in the office at night. The Embassy was near the main bridge over the Nile which led out of the city towards the desert. I confess that on one or two nights when I was performing this duty, I got up every now and then in the middle of the night to watch the traffic going over the bridge and see which way the tanks were moving. Fortunately they all moved west.

We also had to prepare the evacuation of a large number of the

Italian community in Egypt. These numbered some thirty to forty thousand people. They practically all renounced their allegiance to fascist Italy and were allowed to stay at large, forming themselves into a loose and not very effective anti-fascist movement. Since I had fairly good Italian, I was assigned to be in contact with them. There was also a much smaller number of high-grade Italian exiles who made their way by one means or another to Egypt, and wished to take part in more sophisticated action against the fascists. There were also a few who were recruited from the Italian prisoner of war camps in Egypt. One of the few methods of propaganda available to us was the use of Cairo radio. It was uncertain how far transmissions from this station could reach, but it was assumed that while Italian troops were in Egyptian territory, this might be achieved. So we put out a series of programmes, read initially by the Italian prisoners of war who volunteered to do this. We soon heard, however, that these transmissions were not welcomed by the Italians, who described the Italian speakers as traitors to their country, and it was therefore decided that it would be better if the programmes were read by someone who was clearly not an Italian. In the circumstances this meant me. So for quite a period I read papers which we had prepared with the help of our Italian friends, designed to create division and if possible subversion among the Italian troops who might have heard them. We had practically no feedback and so I cannot claim with any certainty that our efforts achieved any notable success. Unfortunately the Italians, like many refugee groups, had a strong in-built tendency to quarrel with each other, the main reason being that some of them were Communist and the others very definitely not. We were at that time rather unsophisticated about the extent of Communist penetration of the political scene in Europe and the reason for the bitterness of these quarrels was not immediately apparent. However it was, on a very small scale, the same quarrel that distracted so many of the resistance movements in Europe, most notably in France, Greece, Yugoslavia and Albania.

Fortunately the plans for evacuating these people and others at most risk could safely be put away after the tide turned in the desert in October 1942. Thereafter the war moved away from Cairo, which ceased to have the political-military role that it had enjoyed previously.

In spite of these dramas, life in Cairo continued remarkably unchanged. We sometimes felt guilty about having as much as we wanted to eat and drink (though the quality of the latter was not very high) and we had to warn each other of the fate of Singapore. The word 'Singaporishness' was coined to describe the state of affairs that we had at all costs to avoid. It was believed, rightly or wrongly, that the insouciance of the population there about the imminent threat of Japanese invasion had contributed to the ease with which the British defences were overthrown. There was virtually no enemy air activity over Cairo, only once or twice a very few bombs aimed at the airforce base just outside the city. We went through the motions of blackouts but not too seriously. On one occasion we were enjoying an evening of highland dancing in a house in the garden city of Cairo when an air raid siren went and we had to close all the windows and curtains. This made it intolerably hot and we moved out into the garden. There when the piper tuned up his apparatus with the usual long notes on the drones, this was mistaken by all the houses round about as the all-clear and the lights went on again, fortunately with no evil consequences.

At one moment it was threatened that there would be shortage of petrol and to forestall this, my wife and I bought a small pony trap which I used to use to go to the office in the mornings. We engaged a small Egyptian boy to sit on the floor and take charge of the pony while I was in the office or my wife was doing her shopping. This went on quite happily for a time but unfortunately, while driving the trap home one day, the boy lost control and wrapped it around a lamp post. Soon after this, the threat of petrol shortage was removed and we could revert to the unlimited use of our cars which we had enjoyed before.

I mentioned my wife. For me personally the most memorable event of my time in Egypt was, of course, that we met and got married there. But the means of her arrival and the course of events following it deserve a separate mention. She was the daughter of John Walter, the last Walter co-proprietor of *The Times*. She had

*Wedding Day, June 1st, 1944, with the two witnesses, Lord Kinross (left) and Robin Fedden. At the Consulate General, Cairo.*

married, in 1937 a young Hungarian banker and gone to live with him in Budapest. Hungary was neutral for some time at the beginning of the war and she stayed on there until about 1941, when the German presence was intensifying. She was asked to work for a clandestine British propaganda organization, and at the same time she started divorce proceedings against her husband. Before these were completed, it became apparent that she had to leave and so she went by train to Yugoslavia, where we were in the last desperate weeks of trying to prop up a regime which would maintain that country's opposition to Germany. She continued in another branch of the propaganda organization, working with pro-western Yugoslav journalists. But the German pressure became stronger until finally Yugoslavia came under attack and she had to leave there by one of the last trains to Greece. Some units of the British forces in Egypt had been – very unwisely, as it turned out – diverted to try to prevent the German advance into that country after the Greeks had seen off the Italians. The British and Greek forces were unable to stem the

German advance and another evacuation took place. Ines got on one of the last ships to leave, which made its way to Alexandria. She then moved to Cairo to work for the Arab News Agency, related to the organization that she had worked for previously, and there it was that we met. There were problems however. The divorce in Hungary was not complete and we had to have recourse to the Swiss diplomatic service, since they were representing British interest in Hungary, to see whether they could hurry the proceedings along and obtain for us proof that the divorce had taken place. Other unofficial means were also used to this end and finally, after two years, the Swiss produced a sheaf of Hungarian judicial documents which gave us the required assurances and enabled the British Consul General to marry us in 1944. We remained married for fifty-three years until she died in 1997.

In the midst of the military and political excitement going on around them, a group of notable British and other poets and writers managed to maintain a remarkable level of intellectual activity and even published a periodical – *Personal Landscape* – vaguely modelled on Connolly's *Horizon*, published in London at about the same time. The best known later, I suppose, was Laurence Durrell, who wrote his Alexandria books after he had left at the end of the war, but was absorbing the experience for them during the time he spent in Alexandria. There were also Bernard Spencer, the poet, Robin Fedden and David Abercrombie. Many of them had arrived in Cairo from Greece, where they had been working in the University or for the British Council. Others were teachers from the Cairo University. They added great distinction to a society which might otherwise have seemed unduly mundane and sometimes almost feverishly brittle.

The city of Alexandria demands a section on its own. Before the war it had been normal for the British Embassy to move some of its personnel to summer quarters in the city, where there was a residence for the Ambassador and a small office for those of the staff who accompanied him. This happened in my experience in 1938 and again in 1939, until our stay was curtailed by the outbreak of war. It was enough to give the flavour of a unique environment. Alexandria was at that time largely Greek in culture and Levantine in its society and in its business enterprise. The cotton crop and the banking services were very largely in the hands of Greeks, the large and important Jewish community, and the British. A number of Egyptians went there too, particularly from the Coptic community, which seemed able to mix more easily with the other elements in the city. Under the frivolous exterior of beach parties and night clubs there were deeper and more lasting elements of considerable interest. The most important literary influence was that of the Greek poet Cavafy, who had been discovered for the West by E.M. Forster and inspired a number of the British writers by his extraordinary power of evoking the genius loci and making it seem almost natural to talk in terms of a continuity in the history of the town from Greek times, through Anthony and Cleopatra, to the more modern Greek Diaspora. The continuity was encapsulated for me by a remark by a Greek acquaintance. When the Labour government succeeded the government of Mr Churchill in 1945, he said that it reminded him of the advent of Christianity in the Roman Empire. And he made it fairly clear which of the two he favoured. Wonderful fish restaurants and occasional excursions by land to Burg Al Arab, a village built as a sort of folly by a retired Englishman in the guise of a Tuscan village dumped down on the edge of the sea at the beginning of the Western desert. One memorable journey was by yacht to the bay of Abukir, in the course of which our Greek host regaled us with stories of his misspent youth. One of these ended with what would now be the most politically incorrect remark, *'C'est la seule des femmes que j'ai eues que je ne salue plus'*. There was also the story of when he finally decided to get married, at which point he sent his *homme de confiance* to tell the then reigning mistress and she threw a priceless vase at his head. (I said no kiss and tell, but these perhaps can be excused as giving a flavour of a life that is now irretrievably past.)

One of the advantages of the war moving away was that by 1944 in the summer we were able to undertake another extensive journey, this time northwards into the Lebanon. For those who do not know the topography, the Lebanon is dominated by a mountain range of the same name running roughly north and south, beginning above

Beirut and ending above Tripoli. By extensive planning, we arranged that horses and mules, accompanied by the necessary muleteers, should meet us at the road-head in the mountains above Beirut and that we should travel northwards keeping as near the tops of the mountains as we could till we were above Tripoli, and then descend to join up again with our cars, which would have been brought there. Remarkably all went well after an uncomfortable first night, when we had to camp in the snow having failed to reach the destination lower down which we had set ourselves. We could not possibly carry enough water for the journey but depended on reaching a water source each night. In the snow we had to try to produce enough drinking water by melting snow on our Primus stove. This is an exceptionally laborious procedure, which I do not recommend. Moreover, although we were not at an excessive height, probably something like 6000 feet, the boiling point of water had become lower so that even having obtained water from the snow, it was next to impossible to cook our rice satisfactorily in it.

Two nights later we were able to camp in great comfort and in some of the most beautiful surroundings imaginable at the source of the Adonis River, where it gushes out of an underground channel and is surrounded not only by copious vegetation, but by many traces of ancient religions which found this spot particularly holy. Higher up, near the peak of the Lebanon range, we came, to our amazement, on a mass migration of butterflies moving from the coastal plain over the mountains into the interior. Then there was the visit to the nomad encampment where the shepherds gave us for breakfast their liban, the local version of yoghurt, and freshly gathered honey. Finally we began to descend above Tripoli, walking almost a whole day through an enormous forest of deciduous woodland until we reached the village of the Shaikh who had arranged our transport. He arrived from Tripoli with hampers of delicious food and drink and we slept the last night on his veranda. Our cars duly arrived and we drove back to Cairo. It is remarkable to recall that at that time, which was before Israel existed, we could drive with virtually no frontier formalities from Lebanon into Palestine, then across Sinai into Egypt.

The journey was recorded in a privately printed pamphlet written by Robin Fedden and entitled *A Voyage through Mons Libanus*, with a cover illustration depicting us in Edwardian climbing gear by Roland Pyin. The subtitle, carrying on the anachronism, reads 'The Journal of a voyage through the more unfrequented regions of Mons Libanus undertaken in An. Dom. 1944 by Mr B.A.B. Burrows, First Secretary at his Britannic Majesty's Embassy in Cairo, and Mr Robin Fedden, Master of Arts, accompanied by their wives, the first females of our nation to penetrate to Ain Srir and Marj Hine, in which is faithfully described the wilderness of Sannine, the sources of the Adonis River, the region of the Qornet Saouda, the great forest of Akkar and sundry other matters of geographical and personal interest, together with many valuable observations upon the nature of mountain travel'.

We finally left Egypt the following year to return to London, where I was to carry out appointments in the Foreign Office. This lasted for the next five years.

CHAPTER 5

# London 1945-50

IT WAS SEVEN YEARS OR MORE since we had been in England. Rationing was still in force and we had nowhere to live. We were lucky enough to find quite soon an only slightly damaged house in Orme Square (and kicked ourselves for ever afterwards for not buying the next door heavily damaged house at the same time. They are now changing hands at over a million). So transport to the office was by the 88 bus or quite often by bicycle in fine weather, into Kensington Gardens, round Hyde Park corner and up Birdcage Walk to Whitehall. One learnt for the first time how hilly London is. It was much harder work coming back up the hill than going down towards the river in the mornings.

I was initially given the job of Assistant in the German Department of the Foreign Office, which also dealt with Austria. This was not so interesting as it sounds because the main work of the pacification and reconstruction of Germany was carried out by a separate Commission and the Foreign Office was mainly concerned with any diplomatic questions that might arise, and longer-term thinking. I became the specialist on Austria and spent an interminable time trying to negotiate towards a peace treaty with that country to which the Russians went on objecting. Both Germany and Austria were governed on the spot by Commissions of the powers which had won the war namely the USA the USSR, the UK and France. Each had a zone of occupation and a sector of the capital cities. It became apparent from a fairly early stage that it was not going to be possible to carry out the planned quadripartite government of the two countries, because the Russians had agendas of their own which did not match those of the other three. It was sad that the wartime allies fell out so soon. We made the best of it by breaking up the Four-Power Commissions and establishing two zones in each country, one administered by the Western Alliance and the other by Russia. I suppose it was, in a sense, the beginning of the Cold War.

In the light of this rather depressing picture, I was not sorry – indeed quite the reverse – when I was promoted some time late in 1947 to be Head of the Eastern Department. This comprised the Arab countries, other than Egypt (which had its own Department) and Iran. It was at this precise moment that the question of the future of Palestine was reaching its head. As a result of all the convoluted diplomacy at the end of the First World War, Britain had obtained a League of Nations Mandate to control and administer this area. We had, only about a year before, issued the 'Balfour Declaration'. This was a unilateral declaration made by the British Government, whose troops were in the process of liberating Palestine from the Ottoman Empire. The declaration stated that the Jews could expect to have a national home in Palestine. The origins of, and the reasons for, the declaration have been discussed at enormous length. The best account of one part of the motivation is in *The Bible and the Sword* by Barbara Tuchman. This describes the curious historical love affair between important elements of British society and the Jews and the belief in the justice of the propaganda which called for the establishment of a place where the Jews could once again feel themselves independent, otherwise known as Zionism. The curious and tragic fact was there was also a number of English people who were entranced by the concept of Arabs as the 'Noble Savage'. I refer to Doughty, Gertrude Bell, T.E. Lawrence, and most of the staff of the Arab Bureau at Cairo during the First World War. The result was that a number of incompatible statements were made to Arab and Jewish leaders during the First World War.

There were two other players who greatly influenced and complicated the situation – France and America. The French had a continuing interest in the Middle East, dating sentimentally, though not historically perhaps, from the Crusades. They had been bitterly aggrieved that we had stolen a march on them over the Egyptian shares in the Suez Canal and then in establishing ourselves in the paramount position in Egypt, which they had believed ought, at least in part, to belong to them. In an incredible example of confusion, rather than duplicity, we made an agreement with them about the future of the States of the Levant, now Syria and Lebanon, which was incompatible with assurances that we had given to the Sherif of Mecca, our chief ally in Arabia, in the war against the Turks. The French were thus able to negate our intentions of placing Feisal, one of the sons of the Sherif, on the throne of a newly independent State of Syria with its capital Damascus. So we made him king of another new country, Iraq, instead, and one of his brothers ruler of the tiny desert kingdom of Trans-Jordan. We and the French then divided the rest of the area between ourselves, the French obtaining a League of Nations Mandate to administer Syria and the Lebanon and we obtaining the same for Palestine. The United States of America were subject to very strong Jewish influence owing to the preponderance of Jewish interests in the intellectual and journalistic life of the east coast.

A new situation, or a serious intensification of an earlier one, arose from the end of the Second World War, since the Jews of Europe who had escaped being massacred by the Nazis became enthusiastic and often militant supporters of the idea of creating out of the 'Homeland' promised them in the Balfour Declaration a fully sovereign and independent state of Israel situated in Palestine. We went through an exceptionally uncomfortable period immediately after the war, in which we were trying to prevent very large numbers of Jews entering Palestine from Europe, because we were convinced that this would be bitterly resisted by the existing Arab inhabitants and would lead to a security situation which we might be unable or unwilling to handle. This made life exceptionally difficult for the Labour Governments, some of whom were by tradition and instinct pro-Zionist.

Other Labour politicians, notably Ernest Bevin, were more concerned at the danger that would be posed to overall British political and strategic interests in the area if the creation of a State of Israel led to a combination of the burgeoning Arab States not only against Israel but also against ourselves for having permitted its creation. There was a particularly painful moment when, at the end of a debate in the House of Commons, a group of Labour members led by Crossman sat on their hands during a division to show their displeasure with the policy being pursued by the Government.

In the end there was a decision by the United Nations by the narrowest of margins that the State of Israel should be set up and we saw no alternative but to remove our military and administrative personnel from Palestine by the quickest possible means so as not to get involved in the war which was now imminent between the new State of Israel and its Arab neighbours. As is well known, the State of Israel, against enormous odds, was successful in this war and established its territory running from the Mediterranean to the tip of the Red Sea.

The Foreign Office has had the reputation of being pro-Arab. I do not think there was much sentimental partisanship, but it was clear that we over-estimated the power of the Arabs to exercise control over the region in which they lived and consequently their importance to us.

The French had, at about the same time, to abandon their positions of control in Syria and the Lebanon, which also became independent states. The democratic regime in Syria which had come into being on the French departure did not last long and it was one of my least pleasant assignments to pay a visit to the military dictator who took power a few years later. Our remaining friends in the area were Iraq and Transjordan, later becoming Jordan, which retained the regimes which we had set up in those countries, except for a brief hiccup in the case of Iraq during the Second World War, when a revolutionary regime set itself up there until shortly afterwards suppressed by us. Iraq, during my time in Eastern Department, was more or less ruled by Nuri Pasha, an Arab who had been an officer in the Ottoman Army during the First World War and retained some old-fashioned views of power and statesmanship. During one of his visits to London, which coincided with a time of more than usual unrest in Syria, he said to me almost casually, 'Shall I take Syria?' I had to rush back to the Foreign Office as soon as I could bring the conversation to an end to put this remarkable proposition to higher authority. Needless to say they were shocked and I had to go back to Nuri to tell him that the answer to his question was 'No'.

Iran also began to go wrong during these years. The Anglo-Iranian Oil Company, later known as BP, held the sole concession for extracting oil and they had almost a state within a state, centred on Abadan some miles up the Shatt Al Arab river which divides Iraq and Iran. They had for years enjoyed a monopolistic position of great benefit to themselves and to the UK. But this was being challenged by a new spirit of nationalism in Iran represented by the coming to power of a fanatical politician named Musaddeq. Initially the demands on the AIOC were for better returns from the oil operation to the Iranian Government. The company were, with hindsight, slow to respond and showed practically no awareness that the situation in Iran was liable to radical change. The further consequences of this situation are dealt with in my next chapter, in which I recount the period when I became involved with them in Washington.

Finally there was another event which, as it turned out, greatly affected my own future career. The Persian Gulf, comprising the Arab Principalities on the western side of that Gulf, had hitherto been within the responsibility of the Government of India, and were treated in much the same way as one of the native states in India. This meant a high degree of indirect rule, with the Government of India responsible for the defence and foreign policy of those countries but not for internal affairs, which were left to the native rulers. In 1947-48 the British Government of India came to an end and India and Pakistan were set up as independent states. One of the consequences of this was that the relations with the Arab Principalities of the Persian Gulf were transferred from the Government of India to Whitehall. This meant to the Foreign Office, since the India Office, which had previously been the Whitehall Department dealing with the Government of India, also ceased to exist. The Foreign Office were somewhat startled at this unusual increase in their responsibilities in an area of which they previously knew little. I was therefore sent on a visit to the Gulf to see what went on there and to write a report for the Foreign Office. The British official then in charge of the area was the 'Political Resident', a member of the Indian Political Service, Sir Rupert Hay. He arranged my programme of visits to every part of the area. My report was apparently so well received that I was appointed to succeed Sir Rupert a few years later, as recounted in the next chapter but one.

Relaxation during this period consisted to quite a large degree in more sailing. This time it was in a more up-to-date vessel, a small ocean racing yacht belonging to friends with whom I sometimes sailed. On one occasion I chartered the boat for a voyage to Spain. It has to be borne in mind that the manifold aids to navigation which now exist had then mostly not been invented or not applied to small yachts. We had learnt on the job a certain amount of coastal navigation by means of bearings on lighthouses and headlands, but while crossing the Bay of Biscay, we would be out of sight of any such useful points for two or three days. So I took it on myself to learn the basic minimum of celestial navigation out of books. This meant fixing our position by taking angles of the sun at midday and if necessary of a star or two as well, applying these to the astronomical tables and using the result to correct the somewhat imprecise estimate of distance sailed, which was obtained by trailing a 'log' behind the boat. We were exceptionally lucky with the weather both on the outward and return journeys. In fact in mid-summer this is not so improbable. The weather in the Bay is likely on the whole to be better than that in the Channel. The navigation turned out well and as light began to grow on our last day, the Spanish coast appeared and we excitedly compared it with the drawing which is provided in the pilot book. We found, almost to our surprise, that it matched pretty well the coastline around our objective, Santander. I must say that a little later in the day we confirmed our route when passing through a group of Spanish fishing boats and asking them which was the way to Santander. To our relief they said keep straight on the way you are going. We were most hospitably received in Spain, where we were regarded hopefully as a precursor of the number of British yachts that used to take part in a race from Plymouth before the war. We left the yacht and went inland to Pampluna, which was celebrating its annual bullfighting jamboree. We were able to see Manolete, one of the greatest matadors of all time. The return journey was uneventful. We were making this time for the French island of Belle Ile, where we

*Mother and child, Ines and Antonia, 1949.*

spent a day before completing our course round the corner of Brittany back to Poole.

While we were in Spain a curious incident occurred. My wife had a strong Spanish connection. Her father had been appointed to the British Embassy in Spain during the First World War and the family had liked Spain so much that they spent almost every summer holiday there for many years afterwards and were all bilingual in Spanish. My wife's two brothers then spent some time in similar appointments in the Second World War. So the family was fairly well known there. One day during our stay at Santander, as we were walking into the yacht club, I was approached by a young Englishman who said he was from the Embassy in Madrid and had to tell me that there was some possibility that a dissident Spaniard, who was in trouble with the authorities, might attempt to stow away on our boat to get out of Spain and escape to England. I was not told what we had to do in this event. Fortunately nothing of the kind occurred. I have often wondered since what we would have done. It would have been a terrible dilemma.

In 1950 I was given the appointment of Head of Chancery at the Embassy in Washington.

CHAPTER 6

# Washington 1950-53

To explain the post of Head of Chancery it is necessary to describe briefly the structure of a large Embassy like Washington. At the top there is of course the Ambassador, who in my time was Sir Oliver Franks. He was not a regular member of the Foreign Service but an academic who had played a large part in the operations of the European end of the Marshall plan, which had contributed greatly to the economic resuscitation of Europe after the war. Under the Ambassador is the Minister and under him the Head of Chancery, who is a kind of office manager for the fairly large number of first secretaries who deal with various parts of the world. Having come from the Eastern Department, I naturally continued my specialization in Middle Eastern affairs, of which there were plenty to keep me busy during these years.

It was of course fascinating to be at the centre of the world of politics, diplomacy and military affairs, but for various reasons it was one of the less successful and less enjoyable of my assignments. We were unlucky with our health at this time, including my contracting diphtheria, which caused a severe shock in American medical circles, where it was thought that this was a primitive disease of peasants which had been eradicated. As I lay recovering in the isolation hospital in Boston, I was visited by teams of young medical students who were brought in to see such an unusual case.

It was the era of McCarthyism, the witch-hunts carried out by Senator McCarthy, who suspected that numbers of the establishment, including many of those in the Foreign Service, were tainted with Communism. This went on for a long time until McCarthy overreached himself by attacking the army in a similar way and was seen off by one of their lawyers in a famous session of one of the Congressional Committees. We had our own troubles at the

Embassy too. Philby and Burgess were members of the staff prior to their being exposed as spies for Russia. One has, of course, to ask oneself how we could be so blind as not to see what was going on. The only credit I can take in the matter is that I joined with Christopher Steel, the Minister, in trying to prevent the appointment of Burgess to the Embassy in Washington, not because we suspected him as a spy, but simply because his unruly way of life and untidy habits of work seemed likely to be disruptive in the workings of our office. However the Foreign Office insisted and he duly arrived to take up his appointment, and I had to exert myself to find work for him to do that would not be upset by his irresponsible attitudes and indiscretion.

The climate too was a disadvantage. This was before the days when air-conditioning was widely adopted and the heat and humidity during the summer were a considerable burden. In fact I sometimes thought that my having survived three summers in Washington was one of the qualifications for my being posted to the Persian Gulf. We sometimes managed to escape for part of the summer to islands off the east coast, and once I went sailing with American friends from Cape Cod to Martha's Vineyard. In Washington I still managed to play some tennis and once when I was playing on a very hot day with three friends from the State Department, one of them wittily said, 'Three mad dogs and one Englishman out in the noonday sun'. Another favourite relaxation was square-dancing, a form of folk dancing originally practised on the frontier but now returned to the suburbs, where we dressed up in mock cowboy clothes and danced to old western tunes and at the directions of a 'caller', who could make up the sequences in which we went through the various figures. This brought us in touch with a number of delightful Americans who were not otherwise on the Embassy calling list, and I became a sufficiently adept caller that in spite of my 'non-American accent' I graduated as a member of the Washington Association of Square Dance Callers. So much so that some years later, when we were engaged in one of our little wars in the Gulf and quite a lot of the world press assembled to find out what was going on, our old friend Sam Brewer of the *New York Times* wrote a description of me in which he said I was without doubt the best square-dance caller east of Suez.

The other defect was that Washington at that time seemed hardly a proper city. A great many of the other people to be met there were transients like ourselves – Congressmen, Senators, members of the State Department, businessmen doing their stint in the Government etc. The monuments were fine and the pictures wonderful but that made it more like a museum. Some of our greatest enjoyment was when we escaped from Washington to travel long distances to other parts of the United States. The excuse was usually to address a group of the Foreign Policy Association, the English Speaking Union or suchlike about British foreign policy, for which they seemed to have an insatiable appetite. These occasions took us right out to the West Coast, down to New Orleans and many points in between, southwest to Tucson and to spend a blissful two days off in Yosemite National Park. The journeys were mostly done by car, but going to the west coast we flew in the Civil Air Attache's de Havilland, which he was taking to show off in some exhibition there. On the return journey we were able to divert a little to fly up and down the Grand Canyon.

Workwise, the major events in which I was chiefly involved were the Korean War and the events in Iran which led to the overthrow of Mosaddeq and the return of the Shah. On Korea we were mostly at one with the Americans, and they were profoundly grateful for our effective military participation in the war. At one point, however, it looked as though the Americans might be too eager to press forward and get themselves involved in direct hostilities with China. The British Government were alarmed at this and wanted to issue a word of caution to President Truman. As luck would have it, the Minister was away on leave and the Ambassador was fulfilling a speaking engagement in the west somewhere, so it fell to me to act on this instruction. I did not have to see the President personally, but conveyed the message through the Senior Official in the State Department. The Foreign Office were complimentary about the action that had been taken but sent a mild reproof to the Ambassador for not having been there to do it himself! The only time I did meet

Truman personally was on a matter of much less moment. Lord Astor, the co-proprietor with my father-in-law of *The Times*, was paying a visit and got invited to meet the President. It fell to me to escort him to this appointment. Mr Truman was very affable but there was a slight difficulty. Although the Astors had only come from North America one or two generations back, Lord Astor found it a little difficult to follow the rather broad middle western pronunciation of the President and the President equally found it hard to catch the clipped vowels of Lord Astor, so that I found myself to a certain extent having to translate between them.

Iran was another matter. Since I last mentioned the subject, the situation had worsened. Mosaddeq had announced the nationalization of the Anglo-Iranian Oil Company and the Shah, feeling that the situation had got out of his control, had departed with his family to Italy. The Americans were no friends of our neo-colonialist position in the Middle East or elsewhere, but were prepared to take strong action to reverse this situation and concerted steps were taken between unavowed representatives of our two governments which led to a counter-coup and made it possible for the Shah's Government to be restored. The price for this was that the Anglo-Iranian Oil Company had to give up its concession for the sole disposal of Iranian oil and was replaced by a consortium in which the Americans played a major part.

The question has been asked whether, with the benefit of a great deal of hindsight, this was in fact the right thing to do. In the light of the Shah's final fall some years later and the installation of the present sanctimonious hierarchy, was the last state of Iran worse than what it would have been if Mosaddeq had been allowed to continue in power? It is a fair question. Mosaddeq seemed impossible at the time and it was a pity to allow a powerful and friendly government to be overthrown, but if he had remained, would the nationalistic phase of Iranian politics have been incorporated in its government in ways that would be less harmful both to Iran and to foreign interests there than what actually happened?

By one of the curious linkages that seem to have tied various parts of my life together, my Iranian colleague in Turkey several years later, General Arfa, told me of the part he had played in the restoration of the Shah. He had retired a little earlier from being Chief of Staff of the army, but when he realized that the counter-coup was in operation, he donned his uniform and marched towards the centre of Tehran. In a square on the way he came on a mob of people in a state of turmoil, so he got up on a platform and harangued them in favour of the Shah and claimed that he had won them back to their allegiance!

In 1952 I was asked if I would like to leave Washington to become Minister at the Embassy in Moscow. Perhaps to the surprise of higher authority, I asked for permission to decline this proposal. I said that I thought that there would not be anything very interesting to do there. The Cold War was already rampant. Therefore it would be impossible to meet any Russians. I knew no Russian and would therefore be confined to reading translations of the Russian newspapers, which I thought could be done equally well in London or elsewhere. A few months later I was offered the job of Political Resident in the Persian Gulf, which I accepted with alacrity.

CHAPTER 7

# The Gulf 1953-58

**1. Introduction**

THERE IS A FULLER STORY of my time in the Gulf than I shall have space for here in *Footnotes in the Sand*, published by Michael Russell in 1990. The following is a shortened version of my account of why we were there and what happened during these five years.

The Gulf States, for whose relations with the British Government I was to be responsible, consisted of the following states: from north to south, Kuwait, Bahrain, Qatar, the seven Trucial States, namely Abu Dhabi, Dubai, Sharjah, Umm al Quwain, Ajman, Ras al Khaimah, and Fujairah, and finally Muscat, later known as Muscat and Oman and now as Oman. With all the states other than Muscat we had treaties which gave us responsibility for their foreign affairs and defence, but no responsibility for their internal affairs. They were technically known as protected states. Muscat did not have a treaty of this kind but usually chose to behave as if it had, and, as will be seen, we had not infrequently to intervene to protect its integrity. All these states were very small in population. By far the largest was Muscat, which was very roughly estimated to have perhaps half a million inhabitants. It may be asked why on earth we had such responsibilities for these tiny states and what British interests were served by our having these responsibilities. To answer this question we have to delve somewhat into history. Until the invention of the aeroplane, Britain's relations with its Indian Empire were maintained by ship. In the first half of the nineteenth century the ships of the East India Company, which then administered India, were not infrequently attacked by pirates in the waters bordering on Arabia when they were on their way to Bombay. The home base of these pirates was in the Gulf, mainly in what later became known as the Trucial States, but which was at that time, with good reason, known as the Pirate Coast. To overcome the pirate threat British Naval expeditions were sent into the Gulf, and, sometimes after naval bombardment, treaty relations were established with most of these little countries, particularly those on the Trucial Coast. These treaties provided that the inhabitants would no longer attack British ships and in return the British would protect them against naval attacks by their neighbours. Similar relations with Bahrain came soon after this, those with Qatar a little later, and with Kuwait not until just before the First World War. The only Western Power which had shown interest in the area before our time was the Portuguese. They had established a position in the Gulf for the same kind of strategic reasons as we had, when they maintained their trading station in India at Goa. They had left the Gulf long before our arrival there. There were however remains of their presence both in Bahrain and in Muscat, where the ruins of imposing buildings were still known as the Portuguese Fort. During my time in Bahrain we received a courtesy visit from a Portuguese warship which had been carrying out a friendship mission at Goa. On their departure from Bahrain, I sent them a farewell message expressing the hope that they would not leave it another four hundred years before paying their next visit.

By the end of the nineteenth century the Ottoman Empire, deprived of most of its influence in Europe, moved its efforts southwards and tried to expand its control of Arabia. This was seen as dangerous from the British point of view, when Germany and Turkey made an agreement which would allow a German railway to be built across Asia Minor and down to the head of the Persian Gulf at Basra. This prompted Lord Curzon, then Viceroy of India, to visit the Gulf and make a resounding declaration of continuing British interest to the assembled tribal leaders at Sharjah in 1903. He said: 'We were here before any other power in modern times had shown its face in these waters. We found strife and we have created order. It was our commerce as well as your security that was threatened and called for action... We saved you from extinction at the hands of your neighbours. We opened the seas to the ships of all nations... we have not seized or held your territory; we have not destroyed your independence, we have preserved it: we are not now going to throw away this century of enterprise.' Following on this new evidence of British interest, attempts were made to define frontiers between the advancing Ottoman colonial power and the territories of the states in special relationship with Great Britain. These negotiations made progress, albeit slowly, and a convention defining the frontiers was on the point of being ready for signature by 1914, when unfortunately the Ottoman empire and Great Britain found themselves on opposite sides in the Great War.

There seemed to be a chain of events which conspired to maintain the importance of the Gulf to the United Kingdom. No sooner had the First War ended, than we began to develop air communications with the Commonwealth and Empire, and the Persian Gulf provided ideal staging posts in friendly territory on the way to India and further east. Then it was oil. The discovery of oil in Iran and then in Saudi Arabia prompted interest in the possibility of oil being found in the Gulf States. By the time I arrived in 1953, Bahrain had for several years already had a small production of oil in its territory and a large refinery which refined oil delivered from Saudi Arabia by pipeline. These enterprises were both under the control of American oil companies. Kuwait was developing a very large production of oil in its territory under the control of a combined Anglo-American enterprise. Discoveries followed in Qatar and then in the Trucial States. There were great hopes for production in Muscat, which would have helped to overcome some of the problems facing that country, but these hopes were dashed for a number of years until finally, long after my time, they were rewarded by important discoveries in the interior.

These developments, of course, made it all the more necessary that we should retain our presence in the Gulf in order to promote stability in which the oil could flow without interruption and hopefully so that British companies would be able to obtain a major share in the profits of production.

The arrangements made by the Government of India to carry out their responsibilities in the Gulf were to assimilate the area, broadly speaking, to one of the native states in India. In these the ruler was responsible for the internal affairs of the State but there was a

Resident appointed by the Government of India who dealt with external relations and could usually exercise some sort of advisory function generally. In the Gulf the Resident was dignified with the title, 'Political Resident' and was assisted by Political Agents in the main places in the Gulf, i.e. Kuwait, Bahrain, Qatar and the Trucial States. The similar official in Muscat was known as Consul-General to mark the formal independence of that state. The Residency was in my time at Bahrain, having moved there from Bushire, a town on the coast of Persia, only a few years before my arrival. The treaties also gave us jurisdiction over most foreigners, including members of Commonwealth countries, of whom by far the greater number were Indians and Pakistanis. We had on the staff a trained legal officer who carried out most of this work and a resident judge to take appeal cases. There were also residual judicial powers vested in the Political Resident in case of need, and I once had to sit in an appeal case since the judge had taken part in the trial at the lower level. It was a case concerning a quarrel between two Indian traders and I was fortunately able to confirm the decision of the lower court without too much difficulty. But it was an unusual assignment for a member of the Foreign Service.

This apparatus was supported at the beginning of my period as Political Resident by three Royal Navy frigates based at Bahrain, a small RAF presence at the Bahrain airport, consisting initially of rather antiquated Anson transport aircraft, and a force which had only just been raised in the Trucial States, consisting of recruits from that area with British Officers in command. Later, as will be recounted, we had to augment these forces with a British Army presence.

It was one of the functions of the Political Resident to travel extensively within the area, so as to demonstrate the interest of the British Government, to get to know the personalities in each place, and to get a personal idea of any problems which had arisen. It was also a tradition that initial visits and those carried out on special occasions should be conducted with a certain amount of ceremony, derived from Government of India practice rather than the normal usage of the Foreign Service. On our initial round of calls on the Rulers, my wife and I travelled on board one of the frigates. On our arrival in the port or off the coast where we were visiting, the frigate would fire a salute of the requisite number of guns (there was a list giving the number appropriate to each of the Rulers according to their importance). There might or might not be a replying salute, in some cases fired from antiquated guns left over from previous battles of long ago. I would then disembark in full uniform (white jacket and trousers plus sword plus solar topee with a spike on the top), and be transported to meet the Ruler. Landing conditions were sometimes primitive. At one of the smaller members of the Trucial States, the drill was to get into the ship's motorboat and approach as near as possible to the beach, at which point we were met by a party of the Ruler's retainers and I had to scramble on to the back of the largest of these and be carried the remaining few yards to the shore so that I did not have to get my feet wet. It was a relief that the press had not yet shown sufficient interest in our goings-on to take a picture of me in this rather un-Ambassadorial posture.

Then came the meal. Tables and occasional cutlery had crept in as part of the modernization of the larger States, but on the Trucial Coast we still stuck to tradition and sat on the ground. Knowing that their guests found it difficult to adopt the correct position with their feet tucked in, our host usually provided a large cushion that we could sit on with our legs behind. The important point was not to show the soles of the feet. The food was standard but nonetheless delicious, a great deal of rice, a whole lamb or sometimes young goat, chickens, eggs. All this was eaten with the right hand only. Our hosts had already learned that we did not care to eat the eye of the animal, as had been the custom earlier, but on one occasion the head of the lamb or goat was picked up by our host and the skull broken on the ground so that the brains were exposed for our delectation. One of the smaller Shaikhs on the Trucial Coast was well known for the excellence of his cooking, and we usually arranged our tour so that we arrived at his fort for lunch. On one occasion we were unable to do this and told him that we had to hurry on to our next destination. He insisted on giving us refreshments nonetheless. So we went into his dining room and found what seemed like the usual enormous spread. After partaking gratefully of this, I ventured to say that we had told him that we would not have time for lunch. He replied with a smile, 'This was not lunch, there was no rice'. It was not customary to discuss business while eating, so if necessary we adjourned after lunch to a smaller room where any necessary talk could be had. It was sometimes a matter of a small affray, a frontier dispute, the prospects for the discovery of oil and any gossip that might be available about the neighbours. There were some strong individuals among them. The Ruler of Sharjah was known as a writer and poet. The Ruler of Abu Dhabi liked to talk not only about world affairs but of the latest scientific developments and world geography. It was also there that we had to accept, without visible signs of distress, having our coffee poured by the man who was generally thought to have poisoned three of the present Ruler's predecessors. It was the brother of this Ruler, Shaikh Zayed, who stood out as the greatest personality in the area. He later succeeded his brother and became the first President of the United Arab Emirates when this Federal structure was set up after our departure. He also bought himself a large estate in Scotland. Sitting on the sand with him one day, I asked him what he would do when the oil came to the Trucial Coast and they all became rich. Would he want to turn his village into a new Beirut? He said he would not and his first endeavour would be to make life better in the desert. I have not been there since to discover how much like Beirut the town of Abu Dhabi became, but I am certain that he was true to his intention and spent a good deal of the new resources which oil brought in improving life in the desert oases by the provision of roads and water.

I cannot give a better impression of our first voyage along the Trucial Coast in November 1953 than by quoting the following extract from a diary which my wife kept. We were travelling on board the frigate *Wren* and for part of the time we were also in company with the cruiser in which the Admiral Commander-in-Chief, East Indies, raised his flag on his visits to the Gulf. He was at this time normally stationed in Ceylon, but came up to the Gulf once or twice a year. My wife had the extraordinary privilege of being able to travel in a naval ship because she had the important function of visiting the wives of the Rulers we called on, who, although never seen outside their own quarters, often played an important part in the affairs of their husbands' possessions. I believe that only one other lady was allowed to spend the night on board one of HM ships. She was the wife of the Commander-in-Chief, Mediterranean.

My wife's diary begins:-

Never have I had a more exciting day. Towards evening it soared right into the realms of fantasy. We went ashore and lunched with the Ruler (of Abu Dhabi). We went in the launch, zig-zagging considerably to avoid the reef. We landed by stepping on to a chair. Between the sea and the fort there was only soft sand so we climbed into Michael Weir's (the Assistant Political Agent) Land Rover and made a swerving dash for it so as not to stick. In this manner we literally dashed up to the Palace, where the Ruler was awaiting us. Close to, the fort took on a very attractive aspect, like a one-storey castle out of a fairy tale. After passing along a narrow passage between the double walls of the fort, the sun blazed down on some high stone steps which led on to a ledge about fifteen feet wide running around two sides of the fort and forming the roof of the first storey. On to this ledge we all climbed and gazed down at the courtyard in the centre. The latter presented a very varied and domestic scene, like that of a small village. There were two donkeys and a horse, chicken and geese could be heard and one or two goats scampered about. Children stood in doorways, busy or idle. On our left the entire wall of the fort rose another six feet and ended in battlements through which one could see the sea and desert and a few graceful date palms. Three camels stood tranquilly patient in the shade. The Ruler motioned us into a cool, dark room built in typical Arab style, with no windows but instead the light and air coming down through vertical slits in the thickness of the wall and ending in stone-backed recesses. The floor was decked with not very good Persian carpets, and sofas and chairs were set against a wall all round the room. Here we sat and talked and drank coffee. Then again through another doorway and a brilliantly coloured feast was spread on a table for us on a rickety carpeted floor. The meal was the easiest of the Arab meals yet. One reached for what one wanted and no more. More hand washing and then back into the first room for coffee, rose water and incense and more talk. The Shaikh has a nice twinkle and a charming face. He is very gentle in his manners as they all are.

When we departed, the Land Rover this time got stuck in the sand and had to be pushed out by a party of the local inhabitants. Back on board the ship, we then went fishing but were disturbed by a fantastic signal from Muscat about pirates. They had been seen in the Gulf and were alleged to have boarded an Indian cargo boat, forced the crew to land in Muscat and made off into the blue. We went on fishing for a bit and I caught two (barracuda), the first two, and the Captain then caught one. It was certainly exciting. We had them for supper and they were really most delicious. Yellow spots, but there must be a local name for them. The sun set in a blaze of green and gold while we were out, the moon rose and *Wren* put on all her lights and they were outlined against a fantastic sky. I don't know when I have been so happy and could have gone on fishing for ever. Beginners' luck, I am afraid, but never mind.

When we got back on board, a delicious pandemonium. Question: do we or do we not give chase to the pirates? A cryptic telegram had been received by the Senior Naval Officer. Bernard and the Captain had the charts out, The Navigating Officer was sent for and calculations began. I listened with a whisky and soda while signals were sent and all possibilities were discussed. Finally it was arranged that we should be picked up in the Commander-in-Chief's launch at Sharjah and taken north to the cruiser for an early interview. To meet this timetable we had to leave at once.

On the next day I set off to visit the Shaikha. She was sweet and so were their two children, such finery as they wore, jewels and jewels. The Shaikha gave me a ring set with a large Gulf pearl. The Ruler took photographs of us with his American machine that prints as it goes, but alas they did not come out, or hardly. We persuaded her to remove her mask but she would only do this for a few minutes and was very shy. The children gazed and gazed and the little girl of nine came and sat close to me and never moved. The little boy had a charming little swagger when he walked about with a dagger in his belt . . .

It was eventually decided that we would disembark and return to Bahrain by air, while *Wren* went off to chase the pirates. It was an important matter to deal with this quickly because, after all, it was on account of piracy in the Gulf that we had originally established our presence there. The Sultan of Muscat, who had a much better local

*New Year's Day reception at the Residency, c.1954.*
*Left to right: Ines, H.H. The Ruler of Bahrain, Antonia.*

intelligence service than ours, was able to tell us shortly afterwards that the ship had put in at a small port on his southern coast. One of the frigates crept in there at night with all lights extinguished but pinpointing the pirate ship by radar and then, when close enough, switched all the lights on, sent a boarding party and overpowered the pirate crew, which was a satisfactory outcome.

The question has to be faced whether all this flummery, the dressing up and eating meals on the floor etc., was really productive of any good or in our interest and whether even in 1953 it was not already antiquated. The answer must be that we were maintaining control of an area of rapidly increasing importance (because of the oil) by means of political influence and minimal force in the shape of the three frigates. The visits to the Rulers and the exchange of gun salutes etc. demonstrated that we continued to respect their position and their ability to maintain order in their own states in their own way. At the same time, the occasional presence of the ships showed that we were ready and able to carry out our side of the bargain, namely to protect them against external attack. Moreover the rule of the local Rulers was on the whole not tyrannical or oppressive. They did not apply the barbarous shar'ia code of law and they respected a version of democracy which was different from ours but nevertheless locally respected as having been in force since time immemorial. This took the form of regular meetings between the Ruler and his subjects. Originally he would sit under a tree, latterly more likely in a mud fort, and anyone with a grievance or complaint against someone else could come and sit with him and speak about it directly to him, whereupon he would normally give a decision. This act of sitting – Majlis – gave its name to the Parliaments set up in some of the Arab States. It is not necessarily the case that the latter were always better than the more primitive versions adopted by the Rulers of the States of Eastern Arabia.

## 2. Bahrain

Bahrain was distinguished from the other parts of the Gulf in three ways. The population was almost equally divided between adherents of the two branches of the Moslem faith, Sunni and Shia. The Shia were probably the original inhabitants but after the arrival of the Sunni Arabs, possibly travelling overland from the Yemen, they tended to have rather a depressed condition in the state This perhaps made them all the keener to celebrate the Shia rites with more than usual intensity. At this time, I think, Bahrain was the only place in which the famous Shia festival of the tenth Muharrem was celebrated in its full rigour, with processions through the town and young men flagellating themselves with chains and cutting themselves with swords.

This manifestation was obviously a source of tension between the two communities and the procession, which took place shortly after my arrival in 1953, set a fuse that had long-term consequences.

The second factor that made Bahrain different was that it had had fairly small quantities of oil for much longer than the other states of the Gulf and had made some extra money by refining oil from Saudi Arabia. The result had been that its development was gradual instead of traumatic as in Kuwait. Education, for example, and medical care were widespread to a fairly high level and the state continued to live from trade as well as simply sitting back and receiving oil royalties. Thirdly, there had been a British advisor in Bahrain since well before the Second World War. He was Sir Charles Belgrave, who had obtained the job by answering an advertisement in a London paper. He had gradually taken over responsibility for the whole of the administration and was greatly valued by the two rulers whom he served. This was good for the orderly progress of the state, but to some extent acted as a barrier between the ruler and his family, on the one hand, and the general population on the other. Belgrave's presence also reinforced the innate conservative tendency of the rulers and made them unaware that the world, and in particular the Arab world, was changing. The very fact that the Bahrainis were better educated made them more conscious of the fact that they had no part in the government of the state and led a few of them to think of ways in which political changes could be brought about. At the same time there was growing influence from the propaganda emanating from Egypt, now under Colonel Nasser. He was quarrelling with us about the withdrawal of British Forces from Egypt and purported to represent a revolutionary idea of society which he wanted to propagate throughout the Arab world. An autocratic traditional regime in close relations with Britain was therefore a prime target for his propaganda machine.

One of the most uncomfortable half hours of my time in the Gulf if not of my life, was spent in the company of Colonel Nasser, when he arrived unexpectedly in Bahrain on his way back from the Bandung Conference in June, 1955. I was woken early in the morning by a telephone message from the airport to the effect that Nasser's plane had been diverted by fog from the airport in Eastern Saudi Arabia where he was due to make a refuelling stop and that the plane was obliged to land in Bahrain instead. The ruler of Bahrain wisely decided that he did not want to receive Nasser but sent Belgrave instead. I had to be there as representing the British Government who were responsible for the foreign relations of Bahrain. Luckily it was still early in the morning when Nasser arrived, and I took him into the airport where we drank endless cups of tea or coffee and made rather stilted conversation. After a certain time, when I hoped that the aircraft might soon be ready to leave, Nasser made the remark which I had been dreading, to the effect that he would rather like to have a look at Bahrain. I was only too well aware that if he was seen in the town, this would lead to all kinds of demonstrations and that the situation might well get out of hand. I debated in my mind whether I could instruct the RAF officer commanding the military side of the airport to have a serious accident to one of his trucks in the gateway of the airport perimeter, thus preventing traffic coming in and out, or whether, in the last resort, I should offer to take Nasser in my car, flying the Union Jack in the hope that he might not find this a comfortable situation.

Fortunately, he did not press the point when I said that I did not think there would be time, and shortly afterwards, to my enormous relief, we were told that the aircraft was ready. The members of the political 'Committee' who were organizing the political movement in Bahrain arrived after Nasser had already gone aboard, but were able to have a short conversation with him in the aircraft.

It soon became apparent that the situation in Bahrain was going to test to destruction our doctrine that we were responsible for the external affairs and defence of the Arab principalities, but not for their internal affairs. One of the weaknesses of Belgrave's administration was that he had not built up the police to a degree that would enable them to keep order in the event of serious disturbances. Moreover, he had retained the position of Commandant of the police, which was quite unpractical in the event of serious emergency, since he would necessarily have had a great many other things to do and could not have led the police force as would be required in the event of serious troubles. I was able to persuade him that the situation needed to be remedied.

This problem was eventually dealt with by the Bahrain government appointing Colonel Hammersley, a former Governor of Sinai in the Egyptian service, to be Assistant Commandant of Police, as well as introducing a number of other British officers and increasing their numbers. In spite of this it was clear to us that we might very well have to intervene in order to maintain order in Bahrain if the political movement became more active. But we sympathized to some extent with the wish of some of the people to have a moderate degree of political reform and unless this took place, we would find it difficult to provide the British forces necessary to back up the police. We therefore got involved in a long-drawn-out argument between the Bahrain Government and the 'Committee' to see whether some accommodation between them was possible.

These discussions were going on with varying degrees of success, when events took a more critical turn. In March 1956 it was announced that the British Foreign Secretary, Selwyn Lloyd, was going to spend a few hours in Bahrain on his way to India. The Ruler arranged to entertain him to dinner. By ill fortune the day of Selwyn Lloyd's arrival was the day on which the announcement was made that King Hussein of Jordan had sacked General Glubb, who had for many years been the Commander of the Arab Legion and who had up till then been regarded as one of the main pillars of the Jordanian state. To the Bahrain activists it was inevitable that the comparison should immediately be made between this act and the position of Belgrave in Bahrain. There had already been popular clamour for his departure and now here was a precedent when another Arab ruler had, at short notice, dismissed his British Adviser. Even so, it is quite possible that nothing might have happened but for the fact that immediately before the Foreign Secretary's arrival there had been a football match in Muharraq, the ground being near the point where the road from the airport takes a sharp turn. This meant that a crowd was already present and gave an excellent opportunity for mobilizing protest.

The positions of Belgrave and Glubb were in some ways similar but in other ways different. What they had in common was that they had both stayed too long in their positions and that this had turned out to be a disadvantage both from their point of view and from the general British point of view. Circumstances had changed so rapidly that the admirable work which they had carried out in the past could no longer be performed in the same manner and a degree of British tutelage which their presence implied was no longer acceptable in the growing spirit of nationalism which was then pervading the whole of the Middle East. They were by no means alone in staying on too long. It has been a fairly widespread failing of politicians and others, from Winston Churchill down.

To understand what followed it is necessary to have a glimpse of the topography of Bahrain Island, which was to play a decisive part in the events of this evening and on subsequent occasions. The main island, in which lies the capital of Manama and at that time the British naval base and Residency at Jufair, is attached by a causeway (built by Belgrave's efforts at an earlier date) to the next largest island, Muharraq, on which the airport and the RAF base and facilities were situated. The road between the two takes a dog-leg turn on leaving Muharraq and joining the causeway before arriving at Manama. The Ruler and Belgrave and other officials and notabilities had gone to the airport at Muharraq to meet Selwyn Lloyd on his arrival by air. We piled into a procession of cars to make the journey back to Manama. When we reached the corner at the end of Muharraq there was a crowd of people on either side of the street and the cars were obliged to slow to almost walking pace. As my car passed, containing the Foreign Secretary and the Permanent Under-Secretary, Sir Harold Caccia, someone threw a handful of sand towards it, some of which came in through the top of the window and landed on Harold Caccia. We were able to pursue the journey without further trouble. The later cars in the procession suffered worse, some at the end having stones thrown at them and one or two people being slightly injured. We all arrived at the Ruler's palace in Manama for dinner. That was only the beginning of the trouble since the crowds by that time had occupied the whole of the road and refused to disperse. We got through the dinner without anyone showing overt signs of perturbation. Belgrave remarks in his book that it was the most trying social function that he ever attended. For once I am inclined to agree with him. When the time came for Selwyn Lloyd to return to the airport for take-off, it was reported by the police that the road was not yet clear and we had to wait. The waiting went on for two or three hours, during which we received periodic reports of what was happening. Finally we were told that the crowds had dispersed and it was possible to leave. The return journey to Muharraq was uneventful and Selwyn Lloyd's party took off a few hours late for his next destination. That the police were able to clear the road, even with this most embarrassing delay, was entirely due to the fact that they had been reinforced on our insistence, and to the personal courage of Colonel Hammersley, who suffered a broken arm in the process, but finally succeeded in the objective of allowing the party to leave without incident. It was a close-run thing and I do not like to think of what might have happened if the police had not received this strengthening during the past three years.

In his book *Suez 1956* (Jonathan Cape, London, 1978) Selwyn Lloyd took a fairly relaxed view of this incident and gave an account of the dinner party in friendly terms. At a press conference during his stay in Bahrain he said that the British Government believed in the gradual evolution of representative institutions and in the maintenance of law and order. The speed of programmes must vary country by country. The British had great confidence in the Ruler.

This incident made us realize that we could not depend on such a narrow margin on further occasions of the same kind and that we must be prepared to intervene with British forces if required in order to maintain law and order if they were threatened to this extent. Only a week or two later another accidental incident provoked further trouble in the streets which the police proved unable to contain without opening fire. This led to a strike and further disorder and the imposition of a curfew which did not prevent a good deal of damage being done to cars and buildings.

After the strike died down, Belgrave and the Ruler agreed to meet the members of the 'Committee' who were more or less managing the political movement and negotiation and discussions dragged on not very fruitfully about the composition of the various councils. There was however one matter on which we felt obliged to intervene, with great reluctance. One of the slogans shouted by the crowd on the occasion of Selwyn Lloyd's visit was the demand that Belgrave should go, following on the dismissal of Glubb in Jordan, and this demand kept on being repeated. From a rather cynical point of view, it was perhaps advantageous to us that the presence of

Belgrave, and the hope that he might be got rid of to some extent, acted as a buffer between the anti-foreign elements in the popular movement and the British authorities themselves. Criticism was focused on Belgrave's position as head of the Ruler's Government rather than on the British presence as such. Nevertheless I came to the conclusion that his continued presence in Bahrain was not serving any useful purpose either for the Ruler or for ourselves and that in spite of all the vast services which he had rendered to the State over so many years, his presence was now an important source of instability and that both Bahrain and the British presence in the Gulf would be better served if he could be persuaded to leave. I put this point of view to London. The Foreign Office then wrote a paper on the Bahrain situation which Selwyn Lloyd submitted to the Cabinet. This included some critical comments on Belgrave and recommended that a new British official should be appointed to take his place. The other recommendations were that we should continue to press the Bahrain Government to meet those of the demands of the reformist movement which we thought acceptable, while at the same time reaffirming our general support for the Ruler.

In a further Cabinet paper a month later Selwyn Lloyd made a more general exposé of British interests and policy in the Gulf. In the interests of maintaining uninterrupted access to the oil resources, it was our objective to preserve internal security and promote good government, social progress and economic development, thus retaining the goodwill of the Governments and peoples. The dangers seemed to be that the Rulers would lose authority, that there could be encroachment from outside or that the administration should degenerate to the level of that in neighbouring states. It was noted at the same time that in Bahrain the opposition political movement seemed to be directed largely at the position of Belgrave rather than at the British authorities as such. I enlarged on these points with particular reference to Bahrain in a minute which I wrote at the Foreign Office later in that year to the effect that while the Ruler was and should be responsible for internal affairs, the British Government had an interest in protecting the interests of foreigners and therefore in ensuring that there was no serious breakdown of law and order. With the growth of the political movement, the choice was whether to repress such activities or to make concessions which were in any case reasonable. Unfortunately the security forces at the disposal of the Bahrain Government had for years been inadequate and the British Government were ready to use British forces if absolutely necessary, but not in any circumstances simply as an adjunct to the Bahrain police. Our advice had accordingly been to strengthen the Bahrain police, to introduce reasonable reforms and to allow the political movement to express its views to the Bahrain Government in a constitutional manner. If the Ruler were stronger, there would be less need for the British Government to intervene.

So far as Belgrave was concerned, the Cabinet accepted Selwyn Lloyd's recommendations in the earlier paper and I was authorized to go ahead and put to the Ruler and to Belgrave himself the view that it would be best if he left in the near future. My interviews for this purpose with both the Ruler and with Belgrave were, naturally, painful. The Ruler was very reluctant indeed to let Belgrave go and Belgrave saw no reason why he should. In the end, however, the Ruler agreed to make an announcement during the summer of 1956 to the effect that Belgrave would be leaving in the New Year. There was, however, hardly the time to enjoy any useful effects which this announcement could be expected to have before Suez was upon us. Although by this time the internal grievances of the political movement had been to quite a large extent removed and their position was much weaker than it had been before, they obviously felt unable to let this opportunity pass. The Bahrain Government agreed to allow a procession of protest and fixed the route for it but, as might have been expected, the agreed arrangements did not work out in practice, a considerable further amount of damage was done to foreign businesses in the island and the situation became so threatening that we had finally to involve more British forces. The sequence of military involvement is described in greater detail in the chapter on Suez below. At the same time, in the new circumstances and in the atmosphere of conflict with Egypt, it became impossible any longer for us to maintain a mediating position or to dissuade the

Bahrain Government from making some arrests. This was done without incident and without adverse security consequences.

The Foreign Office sent on to me a complaint which they had received from the head of the parent company of Gray Mackenzie, the local shipping firm, whose slipway and other buildings and equipment had been badly damaged by the rioters. The complaint was to the effect that we ought to have intervened with British forces earlier in the troubles, so as to prevent this damage occurring. I replied to the Foreign Office that we had acted on the principle that the British should not intervene until it was clear to everybody that such intervention was necessary in the general interest. This was the case after the slipway had been attacked, but might not have been so earlier. I said that our judgement appeared to have been correct since there was absolutely no public reaction against our intervention when it was carried out, and the situation rapidly returned to normal. This argument was accepted in the Foreign Office as valid, but there is no record of whether they were able to convince the company to the same effect.

After this things settled down considerably but the timing of Belgrave's departure still presented a problem. The Ruler hoped that he might stay until the end of 1957, but fate then took a hand and he became seriously ill in the spring of that year. He had to return on medical grounds to England and decided that this should be the end of his service in Bahrain. No new Adviser was appointed. The British official who had been the next senior to Belgrave was given the appointment of Secretary to the Bahrain Government but without the full range of responsibilities which Belgrave had enjoyed. It was a tragedy that he did not leave Bahrain a few years earlier and that his concluding period there was overshadowed by the internal troubles which arose from 1953 onwards, culminating in really serious disorders with which his administration was entirely unable to cope. It is difficult to avoid making a further more general comment not so much on him as on the system which he represented. This was that owing to his presence and the concentration of authority in his hands and because of the very success of the administration which he organized and the progress for which he was responsible in Bahrain over so many years, the local inhabitants from the Ruler downwards became accustomed to think that whatever happened in the island was largely his responsibility and that they themselves did not have any great part to play. It was ironical that one of the first aims with which I was involved, even before I reached the Gulf, was to seek to persuade the Ruler of Kuwait that he should appoint an overall British Adviser, while three years later I had to persuade the Ruler of Bahrain that he would do better to get rid of his Adviser. The contrast with Kuwait was instructive. There the administration was run by the members of the Ruling Family, with a few foreign subordinates. Initially it had problems dealing with the consequences of sudden wealth, but gradually settled down, though never being so orderly as Belgrave's administration in Bahrain. It can of course be said that the vastly greater amounts of money available to the State of Kuwait made it easier to exert authority, if only for the reason that more people had more to lose by any breakdown in law and order and any interruption of the largesse of the state. Nevertheless there was also a more evident robustness in the administration. It is a dilemma which has cropped up all over the world: is it better to be well administered or to administer less well by one's own efforts? Virtually every dependent people has chosen the latter alternative, often with fairly dreadful results. For a number of years Bahrain and Kuwait chose differently.

## 3. Buraimi

One of the most difficult and persistent problems with which I was faced in the Gulf was the absence of well-defined frontiers. In the past the concept of geographically defined land frontiers was alien to most of Arabia. A large proportion of the inhabitants moved long distances following the camel grazing. Their allegiance was to their tribal leader or to the leader of a confederation of tribes, not to a country defined by lines on a map. We had, during and after the First War, settled some of the frontiers in the north, notably those between Kuwait and its neighbours, though that between Kuwait and Iraq was only too obviously regarded as impermanent, as demonstrated by Iraq's actions against Kuwait in later years. But lower down there was an almost complete absence of certainty. Bahrain and Qatar had various obscure minor frontier disputes. The borders between the Trucial States were unmarked and in some cases subject to dispute. These were dealt with in a painstaking process of demarcation undertaken by a member of my staff, Julian Walker, as recounted in his book *Tyro on the Trucial Coast* (Memoir Club, 1999).

More importantly, the Trucial Coast frontier between Saudi Arabia, Abu Dhabi and Muscat was almost totally unknown. As recorded above, we had been on the point of agreeing frontiers in the southern part of Arabia with the Ottoman Government just before the First World War, but these had never been ratified. We later used this quasi-agreement and put forward as a basis for discussion with Saudi Arabia roughly the line that was due to be agreed between us and the Turks, but this negotiation was unsuccessful. The delimitation of the frontiers was nevertheless becoming urgent because of the likelihood that oil would be found in many parts of Eastern Arabia in addition to the finds already registered in Kuwait, Bahrain and Qatar.

The part of the problem that caused far the most trouble and preoccupied me for a good deal of time was the frontier between Saudi Arabia, Abu Dhabi and Muscat, which covered the whole south-eastern area of Arabia.

To understand what this was all about it is necessary to absorb a little of the history and geography. There were two strands to the problem: the first centred on an area called Buraimi. This was a large oasis or group of small oases situated about one hundred miles south of the Trucial Coast. In our view two of the nine villages in Buraimi belonged to the Sultan of Muscat, the other seven to Abu Dhabi. Muscat had at one time been the greatest power in south-eastern Arabia but had come down in the world, partly, it was alleged, because we had suppressed the slave trade and the arms traffic which used to be two of its most profitable enterprises. The rule of the Sultan of Muscat was clear along most of the coastal area of the state, but inland it was much more shadowy. A number of the tribes in the interior also owed some sort of allegiance to the 'Imam'. He was basically and in origin a religious leader but, partly through neglect by the government of Muscat, had acquired a varying degree of temporal power in parts of the interior. The position of the Sultan of Muscat was relatively secure when he had enough money to pay subsidies to the tribes of the interior. However the Sultan with whom I dealt, Said Bin Timur, had inherited from his father a nearly bankrupt treasury and was unable to continue the subsidies on the scale which the recipients thought appropriate. He had let a concession for oil in his territory to a subsidiary of the Iraq Petroleum Company and they were busy exploring, but unfortunately they were unsuccessful for a number of years. This left the Sultan in a difficult position, and laid the Imam and the tribes of the interior open to the thought that they might get a better deal if they allowed the influence of their neighbour Saudi Arabia to increase. The Saudis also had a shadowy claim to Buraimi on the grounds that they had once or twice occupied it in the course of raiding in that direction. It was also alleged that it had been an important way station in the slave trade, which had resulted in many scores of Africans being sold as slaves to the Saudis and other tribes further north. It was also alleged that the then King of Saudi Arabia, Saud, had a special regard for Buraimi since he had been there as a young man.

However all this may be, the Saudis precipitated trouble by sending a small military party in 1952 to occupy the two villages in Buraimi belonging to the Sultan of Muscat. The facts of geography have to be borne in mind in assessing these claims and counter-claims, the most important being that Buraimi is four hundred miles of waterless desert away from the nearest Saudi habitation. It was often alleged that part of the reason for the Saudis making this claim in so dramatic a fashion was that there were large reserves of oil in the neighbourhood of Buraimi, and it was sometimes added that the Arabian American Oil Company (Aramco) was pushing the Saudis to expand their territories so that they could obtain even larger reserves of oil than they already had in the rest of the country. I do not believe that oil was a significant part of the motivation. There was no compelling evidence that there was any significant quantity in the neighbourhood of Buraimi and none has in fact been found there since. Aramco may well have said that if Saudi territories were extended in this area, they would naturally be glad to explore for oil there, but I doubt if it went much further than this. More likely, the motives were plain old-fashioned imperialism, with the simplistic geographical view that since Saudi Arabia was the largest state in the Arabian peninsula, it ought to have control over the whole geographical entity. Much the same in fact as the 'manifest destiny' of the early Americans to expand from coast to coast.

There was possibly another circumstance which pushed some of the Saudi Government's advisors to promote this extension. The Egyptian military had just carried out the last phase of their revolution and got rid of King Farouk. The Saudi and other monarchies in the area must have felt this might be a dangerous presage for them. It was also a time at which the British were beginning their difficulties with the Egyptians over the position of the British Forces in Egypt and the control of the Suez Canal. It may possibly have seemed that if the Saudis were making an anti-British move, this would go a little way towards ingratiating them with the new Egyptian regime.

Whatever the reasons, the Saudi detachment in Buraimi started trying to expand their influence among the local tribesmen, mainly by handing out large sums of money. This was too much for the Imam, who may previously have been receptive of the idea of some Saudi help towards his greater independence but did not like the prospect of being ruled by a Saudi outpost in Buraimi any more than that of being ruled from Muscat. He therefore appealed to the Sultan of Muscat to help in a joint project of turning the Saudis out of Buraimi and said he would raise the tribal forces under his influence to take part. The Sultan moved up the coast from Muscat and was poised to lead a tribal movement towards Buraimi when unfortunately he was told by the British Government that he should not do this and that if he complied, they would help him to regain his influence in other parts of his dominions.

This all happened more than a year before I arrived in the Gulf. From the papers in the record office it is clear that these instructions derived personally from Mr Eden, who was then Foreign Secretary. The main reason appears to have been that while acute troubles were building up in Egypt following on the Egyptian revolution, the last thing he wanted was that Britain should be involved even indirectly in an armed incident with another Arab State. The Sultan had not asked for British help except in stopping further movement of the Saudis into what he alleged was his territory, which indeed might have seemed a reasonable request in the light of our general relations with him and our obligation to protect his neighbour Abu Dhabi against foreign attack. But the instructions to my predecessor became ever more pressing and, and one might almost say, passionate and finally the message had to be transmitted to the Sultan by the Consul General. The Sultan rightly insisted on having the message put in writing so that he could show his followers that he was acting under *force majeure* from the British, on whom ultimately he depended for his protection. The Muscat and Omani forces were then dispersed and after an acrimonious argument between us and the Saudis, we agreed with them to set up an arbitration process to decide on the ownership of the villages in question. This provided for the continued existence of the Saudi detachment in Buraimi and the presence of a British-sponsored unit from the Trucial Oman Levies in another village, and for restraint on both sides in trying to extend influence or supply arms. This provision was particularly important because it was anticipated that the arbitration process would include some form of ascertainment of local opinion.

In a cabinet paper of 1952, after he had stopped the Sultan of Muscat from driving the Saudis out of his territory, Eden set out some of his reasons for doing so and for concluding that arbitration was the only way of solving the problem. He started off by saying it was unacceptable that the Muscati forces should come into conflict with the Saudi forces and suggested that the only alternative was for a great deal of money to be spent on buying support from the tribes of the interior. This money would have to be provided by the British Government. He was under no illusions about the probable results of arbitration. He suggested that the Abu Dhabi case was strong but Muscat's considerably weaker, since the authority of the Sultan had

*Wind towers at Dubai, Trucial States.*

not been exercised in his villages for a considerable time. Nevertheless he thought that the results of arbitration would be better for Muscat than to leave matters as they were, with creeping increase of Saudi influence. It was one of my first duties, on arriving in the Gulf, to visit the Sultan in his southern home at Salala in the extreme south west of his territory and persuade him to agree to the formal proposals for arbitration. He did so with great reluctance.

Salala was a beautiful place, almost more African than Arabian in aspect. It was one of the very few places in Arabia, apart from the Yemen, which received the monsoon rain. This meant that after the rain the countryside was covered with tall grass and there were lakes and waterfalls. By agreement with the Sultan, the RAF maintained a small station a little way inland from the sea, to which I flew on numerous occasions. The navigational aids were sparse. One was warned that if one had to fly there in monsoon weather, the drill was to approach from the sea, in the belief that it was almost always possible to see the line of surf on the coast, but the monsoon conditions set in immediately thereafter with practically no visibility.

*With the ruler of Ajman, Trucial States.*

Therefore after crossing the surf, the aircraft flew on for a very limited length of time and if it had not seen the airfield at the conclusion of that time, it had to do a 180 degree turn and abort the journey altogether. Fortunately this never happened to me. There was nowhere to stay except in the Sultan's guesthouse. He maintained an Indian cook to look after foreign visitors. Breakfast consisted, rather idiosyncratically, of porridge followed by tinned salmon, accompanied by the delicious local bread and honey. At other meals I partook of the Sultan's generous hospitality. He took me driving in his Jeep station-wagon to see the beauties of the countryside after the rain. The only disconcerting feature was that whoever had taught him to drive seemed to have told him that on descending a steep hill he should put the clutch out, so that one had no braking effect from the engine and depended entirely on the brakes.

Returning to Buraimi. Fortunately, as it turned out, the Saudis could not restrain themselves from overreaching the terms of the agreement. They distributed large sums of money and sponsored action by their supporters among the local population so as to extend the area of their control. In 1955 this thoroughly unsatisfactory situation finally led London to break up the arbitration and to authorize me to recover Buraimi by force. This was achieved by a force of the Trucial Oman Levies (local soldiers with British Officers), with remarkably few casualties. The Saudi officer in command of their detachment was wounded in the behind by a revolver shot when he tried to grapple with the British Officer, who penetrated into his headquarters and invited him to surrender. He was moved to one of the British frigates lying off shore and treated there for the wound. Some days later he returned to Saudi Arabia. The authority of the Sultan of Muscat was restored in his two villages and that of Abu Dhabi to the remainder was confirmed. The Saudi reaction was not so serious as might have been expected. I was approached not long afterwards by two intermediaries, who indicated that they wanted things to return to normal as soon as possible. An important part in the success of the battle was played by Edward Henderson, a member of the oil company who was seconded to my staff, and who set up a presence in the outskirts of one of the villages in Buraimi. Here he received visits from various leaders of the villages and eventually persuaded those who had sided with the Saudis that the time had come for them to switch back to their former allegiance. He wrote an account of this story in his book *This Strange Eventful History* (Quartet Books, London, 1988). The Buraimi question was finally brought to a friendly conclusion in 1974-5, long after I had left the Gulf, by means of the cession by Abu

Dhabi to Saudi Arabia of a small area of sea coast in return for Saudi acceptance of the status quo at Buraimi and their relinquishment of their claim to it.

One of the most extraordinary features of the Buraimi affair was that this tiny battle in a village on the edge of the empty quarter gave rise to, or more properly was believed to give rise to, feelings of indignation in high quarters in America. The Americans cherished their relationship with Saudi Arabia and at that time took pride in the fact that they were able to maintain it without having American forces stationed in or near the area. This, they held, was in contrast to our difficulties with Egypt, because we tried to insist on keeping our forces there when the Egyptians did not want this. But in my opinion, Eden greatly exaggerated the effect on the United States of this particular aspect of our relations with Saudi Arabia. The day before he resigned in 1957, Eden wrote a short cabinet paper rebutting one by Macmillan, who had said: 'The Suez Affair has been a tactical defeat'. Eden tried to claim that it had not been a wholly disastrous affair and went on with the words: 'It may be that the United States' attitude to us in the Middle East dates from our refusal to give up Buraimi'. Behind this extraordinary remark lies a whole history of antagonism between Eden and the American Secretary of State, Dulles, whom he accused of undermining our position in the Middle East owing to American prejudices against 'Imperialism'. In a letter to me of early 1991, in reply to my sending him a copy of my book, Julian Amery, a right wing Conservative MP and one time Under Secretary at the War Office and son-in-law of Macmillan, said: 'I find the chapter on Buraimi particularly interesting. It was, I suppose, the last Anglo-American war, and we won! The modern UAE (Union of Arab Emirates) and Oman are the result. Towards the end of his life Harold Macmillan came to the conclusion that Buraimi and Oman were really the most constructive things, from our national point of view, that he achieved.' If he really said this, Macmillan was being anachronistic about Buraimi, since this took place well before he was Prime Minister. The termination of the Oman question took place after his accession to power.

In spite of these remarks, I still find it difficult to accept that our two very local incidents should have played this sort of part in the world balance of power.

**4. Oman**

It might have been thought that with the reoccupation of Buraimi and the reassertion of the sovereignty of the Government of Muscat at Nizwa and in other parts of the interior, the situation there could have been regarded as having been restored to tranquillity and its proper and traditional allegiances. This proved not to be the case and the respite was not very long before we had to do the whole thing over again. It is worth devoting a little time to considering why this was so. Without wishing altogether to excuse ourselves or the Sultan of Muscat for miscalculation, it must be said that a large part of the reason for the renewal of unrest in the interior was the failure to find oil. The Iraq Petroleum Company, which held the concession for oil operations throughout the territory of Muscat (other than Dhofar), had been working for some time at a very promising site in the interior at a place called Fahud. All the geology was right and expectations were high that oil would be found in reasonable quantities as soon as serious drilling could be undertaken. The site was in an uninhabited area and work was therefore not unduly disturbed by the political and military goings-on in the rest of the territory. It was the expectation of the discovery of oil in this area which led the British Government to encourage the Sultan to reassert his authority in the interior. It was also the belief that oil would be found which persuaded us and the Sultan himself that the revenue would by that time be beginning to flow and the resulting resources of the state would be enough both to carry out development and improve communications. This would render the inhabitants contented with the new situation and provide the financial support necessary for any increase in the Muscat Defence Forces. There would thus be a more lasting basis for the exercise of governmental authority throughout the territory.

Unfortunately it turned out that the oil company's projections were wrong. The geology might be all that was required but the oil was not there. This radically altered the situation. The tribes of the interior had not liked being under the influence of the Saudis when they were in Buraimi nor under that of the Imam, but it soon turned out that what they really wanted was not to be under any government at all. The prospects of development which they had believed would follow from the reassertion of the Sultan's sovereignty were not realized owing to the lack of resources. The administration of the Muscat Government was ramshackle and the most obvious manifestation of the Government's presence was in its least popular form, that of the tax-gatherer. At the same time external events began to press once more. The Saudi Government continued to be heavily under Egyptian influence and this was reinforced by the Suez campaign. A training camp was set up in eastern Saudi Arabia in which a few hundred Omanis were given some rudimentary training and supplied with better military equipment than they usually possessed. This group became known as the 'Omani Liberation Army'. It was not very long before they made their presence felt in Oman. It is not clear whether the Saudi authorities deliberately sent them into Oman in order to bring about the independence of that area or its transfer of allegiance to Saudi Arabia. Later speculation was that they might in fact have got rather tired of having to support the Omanis in Saudi Arabia and decided to send them home with the arms which they possessed. In any case they succeeded at least in showing up the weakness of the Muscat administration through the fact that they were able to make a landing on the Batinah coast on 14 June 1957 and penetrate a considerable distance inland without being detected. They were, moreover, able to establish themselves in half a dozen villages in the interior and this was symptomatic of the fact that pacification had not been thoroughly achieved. It must have been about this time that I encountered a minor and rather bungled terrorist attempt to disrupt a visit which I was paying to Muscat on board one of the naval frigates. We were due to go on shore to have dinner with the Foreign Minister and, while waiting on deck, heard an explosion from the town. A message arrived that a bomb had been detonated against the outside wall of the Foreign Minister's house, but that no very serious damage had been done, and so far as I remember we were able to have dinner there as planned after the mess had been cleared up.

The Sultan tried to deal with the situation in Oman by sending a tribal levy to contain or expel the Liberation Army, but this was unsuccessful owing to the concentration of fire to which they were exposed from a fort. The Sultan then sent the Oman Regiment, one of the forces which he had recently organized consisting of local troops under British officers. For reasons no longer entirely clear, this force was also unsuccessful. The gun which they took with them was unable to demolish the fort and they were then themselves put into difficulty by the mining of some of their vehicles and they risked being cut off from their base. The regiment was accordingly withdrawn to the oil company camp at Fahud, where they were sufficiently removed from the scene of action to be out of danger. The Sultan then asked for the help of the Royal Air Force but, on the basis of existing policy decisions, this was initially refused. On 16 July, when the situation was clearly deteriorating quite rapidly, he repeated his request for all possible help by land and air and this time the British Government agreed and made a public announcement to the effect that they would provide assistance. The announcement in itself helped to stop the spread of disaffection and shortly afterwards RAF action was taken against the forts in the rebel-held towns and villages. This was strictly limited to rocket attacks on military objectives and it appeared afterwards that only three civilians had been wounded. Leaflets were dropped on the target areas before attacks were made. At the same time a concentration of local forces consisting of the Muscat Frontier Regiment, whose morale was still satisfactory, and two squadrons of the Trucial Oman Levies at Ibri were successful in containing anti-Government activity to the area of the six villages. However it became clear by the end of July, when a senior British officer had arrived from England, that these local forces were unlikely to be able to re-establish control rapidly in the disaffected areas and the recommendation was made that British land forces would have to be committed in order to speed matters up. This was approved in London on 30 July and a rifle company of the Cameronians and a troop of armoured cars of the 15th/19th

Hussars and ancillary signallers etc. were assembled by airlift from Kenya, the Aden Protectorate and Cyprus by the 5/6 August. They proceeded to move southwards from Ibri, planning to make a junction with a force of loyal tribesmen moving north from Muscat who would be prepared to take over the control of the rebel villages once they had been freed. There was initial resistance at Firq, the first village to be attacked. This was reduced by air attack and the position was captured on 10 August, followed by the reoccupation of Nizwa and a junction with the Muscat forces and tribesmen by 12 August. This was followed by the reoccupation of the remaining villages. The main problem for the British forces, apart from the small battle at Firq, was the intense heat of Oman in mid-summer. There were initially some cases of heat exhaustion but the troops appeared to acclimatize quite quickly and suffered virtually no casualties.

A feature of the campaign was that on the approach to villages or towns which might contain inhabitants hostile to the Sultan, the leading detachment was preceded by the figure of Group Captain Jasper Coates (who had previously been Officer Commanding RAF at Bahrain and then entered the Sultan's service, subsequently taking a prominent part in establishing the first naval forces of the Sultanate). He marched forward carrying a large red flag of the Sultanate. In many cases this courageous initiative, backed of course by a relatively large concentration of British force, was sufficient to secure the ending of resistance and the return of the locality in question to the allegiance of the Sultan.

The fortunes of the Liberation Army and the course of events in the area followed fairly closely the assessment by the inhabitants as to which was likely to be the winning side. The initial discomfiture of the Oman Regiment led to an increase in the support for the Liberation Army, in the belief that they could establish themselves against the authority of the Muscat Government; but afterwards, when it became clear that British forces were going to be engaged in support of the Sultan, the contrary effect was produced and there was a fairly rapid scramble to return to allegiance. On this occasion there was a sounder hope of benefits to be received from such a course since, at last, some oil had been found in the territory of the Sultanate. This was not in Oman but in the far south-west, where an American company had been prospecting in Dhofar and announced the discovery of oil in saleable quantity.

On the British side the campaign was enlivened, if that is the right word, by the presence of a number of British journalists who appeared to see in a little desert war the possibility of filling their silly season columns and moved post haste to the Gulf. There were at one time twenty-five British and American correspondents milling about between Bahrain and Sharjah, where the RAF station was the forward base of operations. They were unable to get to the 'front' and could get little hard news except what we rather reluctantly released. They filled this out with more lurid details obtained from returning RAF pilots and complaints at the alleged unwillingness of the British authorities to provide them with better facilities and fuller news stories. This so annoyed the authorities in London that I was told to announce that press releases would no longer be made at Sharjah but only at Bahrain, in the hope that this would secure the movement of the majority of the correspondents from Sharjah to Bahrain, where there would be less scope for them to obtain eyewitness accounts. This was in retrospect an unwise decision and naturally infuriated the press, several of whose members then proceeded to attack my handling of the public relations part of the exercise. There was a basic difference of objective: we wanted to emphasize that it was only a very little war and of very short duration in order that opinion outside the Gulf should not be mobilized against us. The press, on the other hand, wanted something to justify their presence in the Gulf and stories to fill the largest possible amount of column inches under their by-line. Also the Sultan, with his well-known aversion to publicity, refused to see the British correspondents and naturally they blamed us for this as well.

The only relevant external involvement was that the Arab League debated the question of submitting the matter to the United Nations. Action was delayed by the helpful attitude of the Iraq Government. (This was a year before the Iraqi revolution.) In the end they tried to have the question inscribed on the agenda of the

*Hawking on the Trucial Coast.*

Security Council; the Sultan telegraphed to the Secretary General saying that what was happening in Oman was an internal matter and therefore unsuitable for discussion by the United Nations, and the attempt to have the matter raised in the Security Council was defeated.

The British forces had practically completed their evacuation from Muscat by 19 August and on 22 August it was possible to announce the final casualties of the operation, which were one soldier of the Trucial Oman Levies killed and two wounded, two members of the Muscat forces wounded, no British casualties and an estimate of about thirty Omani rebels killed.

The Government in London clearly welcomed the rapid and successful conclusion of these operations as refuting the earlier criticisms in the press to the effect that there was muddle and uncertainty in the conduct of this little war. What the press were really complaining about was the lack of facilities for themselves and the playing down of events by British spokesmen anxious to keep the public aspects of the operations confined to as small an area as possible so as not to provoke political difficulty from the Arab League, the United Nations and the outside world generally. Duncan Sandys, the Minister of Defence, visited Bahrain on 14 August on his way to Australia and in talking to the press at Bahrain Airport, as reported in *The Times* of 15 August, 'offered public congratulations to Sir B. Burrows and Air Vice-Marshal L.F. Sinclair', the Air Officer Commanding at Aden who had been in general charge of the military aspect of the operations, for the 'quiet efficiency' with which they had carried out the Oman operations. According to *The Times* Mr Sandys rebutted 'armchair critics in London who had complained of muddle and delay in Oman; he had no hesitation in saying that the situation had been tackled in the most admirable manner and was a superb example of the way political-military operations of this kind should be handled'. He went on to say that it would have been easy to clean things up more quickly by using a lot of forces and killing a large number of people but through the exercise of patience and restraint Britain had managed to give the Sultan the support he needed at the minimum cost in lives. On the following day *The Times* published a telegram sent from the Prime Minister (Mr Macmillan) to me and Air Vice-Marshal Sinclair in the following terms: 'Now that the Sultan has re-established his administration in Oman and the withdrawal of British forces will shortly begin I should like to congratulate you both on the rapid success you have achieved and on the way you have handled the affair from the beginning. I know that it has been an anxious and trying time for both of you but you have done extremely well and we are all grateful to you.'

The Americans were not unnaturally unenthusiastic, though they do not appear to have expressed their views so forcibly as on previous occasions relating to our activity in Oman. A letter from the British Ambassador in Washington of 10 November 1957 attempts to give some reasons for their attitude, which I am sure was an accurate account at the time, but in the light of later events elsewhere reads in part rather curiously. He said that there was an instinctive American dislike and disapproval of the use of armed force. There was also an anti-colonial complex which made it appear more reprehensible for a white to shoot a black than vice versa (except in certain circumstances in the deep South). Part of the reason was that such action gave a handle to Soviet propaganda. Another part of the reason was that they disliked the use of force which was outside their control because they felt that in the last resort they might have to pick up the pieces in defence of the West.

In spite of the euphoria attending the rapid conclusion of the Oman campaign, it soon turned out that this was unfortunately not yet the end of the matter. A small pocket of resistance was established on the summit of the Jebel Akhdar and was maintained there for another year owing to the inaccessible character of the mountain and the willing or unwilling support of the few inhabitants in the upper reaches. The final denouement occurred after my departure from the Gulf.

## 5. Conclusions

In retrospect what were our purposes during the time that we had responsibility in the Persian Gulf, that is to say from about 1820-1971, and how far did we achieve those purposes? We should finally consider why we decided to give up the system which had existed during those years Our motives were the usual mixture of self-interest and regard for the welfare of people to whom we had obligations, and for whom we therefore had a certain, in this case rather limited, degree of responsibility. The self-interest was obvious, particularly in the later years, namely the creation or maintenance of sufficient stability to ensure the orderly production of oil and use of the money which came from it so as not to upset the financial system which we were trying to direct. This fortunately coincided with a rational view of how the countries of the Persian Gulf could make the very difficult transition from the Middle Ages to the 20th century and from fairly dire poverty to unimagined riches. It seemed fairly clear that it would be of advantage to them as well as to us if this were achieved in comparatively orderly stages, by evolution rather than revolution, and we believed that we could help to insulate them from the currents of revolution and anarchy which were becoming the normal methods of change in many other parts of the Middle East.

We were able to achieve this more successfully because of the limited nature of our responsibility. We were obliged, whether we liked it or not, to exercise a fairly extreme form of indirect rule rather than colonial administration. We were not in all cases to maintain the 100% purity of this distinction, particularly in the case of Bahrain. But it meant that we did not feel ourselves obliged to try to introduce the Westminster model of parliamentary democracy, as we did in almost all other territories which we controlled in Asia and Africa. With the amazing exception of India and a few smaller territories, this system has failed to maintain itself in the face of tribal and other pressures to which the territories have been subjected on gaining independence.

The only countries in the Middle East in which the existing regimes have not been upset in the period since the Second World War are Saudi Arabia, Jordan and the Arab States of the Gulf (with the exception that Kuwait was overthrown by Iraq but its regime was subsequently restored). It is easy to say that in Saudi Arabia and the Gulf States the regimes have found it easier to maintain themselves because of the vast amounts of money which they have been able to hand out to the population, but it is hard to avoid the alternative thought that the Bedouin element in the societies of these states contributed a factor of stability. There is a patriarchal tradition among nomad people, and an element of democracy of another kind inherent in the tradition that the Ruler is open to approach by any individual who wants to express an opinion or seek redress for a grievance. One has to be wary of bias here, because the British have always found it much easier to get on with the Arabs of the desert than with those who inhabit the towns and acquire a higher degree of sophistication. We in the Gulf had trouble enough with Saudi Arabia over some of the disputed frontiers, but the more insidious danger was that resulting from the propaganda of the revolutionary regime in Egypt under Colonel Nasser, which attacked not only the British position in the area but also the nature of the regimes.

*Mud-brick fort on the Batinah coast, Muscat, c.1957.*

Overall, it could perhaps be claimed that the later years of our presence in the Gulf gave to the peoples there a breathing space during which they could make calmer choices of their own future than were available to the majority of their neighbours.

We gave up our special position in the Gulf in 1971 for three main reasons. One was the desire to reduce overseas commitments resulting from the defence review, because of our growing lack of resources both financial and military. Secondly, the then Labour Ministers found it repugnant to be seen to be supporting shaikhs, apparently in the rather naive belief that the alternative to this kind of regime would be nice Westminster-style democracy rather than bloody revolution as in Iraq. Thirdly there was the more realistic difficulty of getting there. With an unfriendly Egypt, Libya and Syria, it became increasingly difficult to exercise our previous habit of moving forces in and out of the Gulf as necessary. I was myself forcibly struck by this difficulty in 1961, when there was an earlier Iraqi threat to Kuwait. We concluded that in order to defend Kuwait

*Muscat, 1957. Left to right: Colonel Street, the Rt. Hon. Julian Amery, MP, His Highness the Sultan of Muscat, the author, Leslie Chauncy, Consul General, Muscat.*

we had to have some military aircraft in the Gulf and there was no means of getting them there except to fly from Cyprus over Turkey and down the river valley to Kuwait. I was, by that time, at the Embassy in Ankara and I had great difficulty in securing the agreement of the Turkish Government that aircraft from Cyprus could overfly Turkey for this purpose, because of the presence of numbers of ethnic Turks in Iraq who they felt might be penalized if it was known that they had contributed in this way to our action against Iraq.

The longer-term solution proposed to this difficulty was the rather far-fetched attempt to create an 'all-red' route round Southern Africa, by which we could send ships and aircraft from the UK to the Gulf or elsewhere in the Middle East without having to obtain foreign permission. This foundered for the ridiculous reason that one of the staging points, in an uninhabited island in the Indian

Ocean named Aldabra, was found to be vital to the life cycle of a rare turtle. There was an uproar among the wildlife enthusiasts, who claimed that the establishment of an airfield on the island would be disastrous for the future existence of the turtles.

So, for a mixture of these reasons, we decided unilaterally in 1971 to give up our special position in the Gulf and the treaties we had with the various states. It is one of the very few instances in which our abandonment of part of our imperial heritage has taken place against the wishes of the local inhabitants rather than, as in most others, because we were unwilling to spend the resources necessary to maintain our presence when we were evidently not wanted. It is ironic that a number of years later, when Iraq invaded Kuwait, the United States, which had earlier carped at our responsibility for protecting these states, decided that it was in its interest to undertake, with us and the French, the restitution of Kuwait to independence, just as if they had had the same relationship with Kuwait as we had once had.

## 6. Postscript

In the early summer of 1958 I left Bahrain for London on leave, thinking that I would almost certainly not return, since I had already received the appointment to be Ambassador in Turkey later in the year.

However, when I was at home working on the harvest at Steep Farm, the Iraqi Revolution broke out, resulting in the overthrow of the regime, the death of the King and Nuri and the establishment of a republican regime. I was immediately told that I should return to the Gulf temporarily in order to reassure people there, particularly the Kuwaitis, who might well be feeling that the new regime in Iraq would be more hostile to them than the previous one. There was a problem of getting there. The normal air route to Kuwait would have passed over Iraq, which in present circumstances was impossible. I therefore had to make a detour via Iran. This presented a ridiculous little problem because Iran had a long-standing claim to the ownership of Bahrain, which was the seat of my main office in the Gulf. In their eyes I ought to be an Iranian rather than a British official. I was therefore rather a non-person as regards transit through Iran. Things were smoothed out by the Ambassador in Iran telling the Foreign Minister unofficially what the circumstances were, and getting his agreement that I could pass through provided this was done discreetly. So I flew to Tehran and was whisked away from the aircraft to the Ambassador's summer residence outside the city, where I spent the night, and then made a very uncomfortable flight the next morning in an Iranian aircraft directly to Kuwait, without passing over Iraq territory.

When I arrived at Kuwait, the Ruler was away on his summer holidays. His cousin, Mubarak, was acting Ruler and was in any case in command of the exiguous armed forces of the state. He had set up headquarters in a series of tents at the airport, where we conferred. There was considerable hubbub and at one point, when he wanted to be particularly confidential, he invited me to move into his bedroom. With, I hope, only a momentary flicker of doubt, I complied with the invitation and our conference continued more peaceably. Among his entourage was the son of a former tribal chieftain in southern Iran with whom we had had dealings at the beginning of the First World War, and who now lived in exile in Kuwait. He put to me the splendidly nineteenth-century question: 'Shall I raise the tribes?' It was, sadly, to be doubted whether he in fact had the power to do any such thing and I had to tell him as politely as I could that I did not think it would be necessary. Having done my best to reassure the Kuwaitis that our support remained as reliable as ever, I went on to Bahrain and spent the next few weeks there until the situation in Iraq had somewhat cooled down. Only then did I take my final departure. After a brief further spell in England, we left for Turkey.

Before getting there, however, I feel bound to burden the reader with an account, as seen from the Gulf, of the Anglo-French invasion of Egypt in 1956, which had a potentially dramatic effect on that area, as well as on international relations generally.

CHAPTER 8

# Suez

THE FIRST INTIMATION I HAD of the impending gravity of the Suez situation was when, shortly before my return to Bahrain from leave and consultation in the late summer of 1956, I went for an interview with the Foreign Secretary in his office. Lying on the table at which there had just been a meeting of ministers were printed papers bearing the security classification 'UK Ministers' eyes only'. I was deeply shocked at this apparent mistrust of Foreign Office officials by the Foreign Secretary and it was the first and last time I saw papers with this classification. Civil servants are always apt to be suspicious or anxious when they know that ministers are running free, that is to say are operating or planning to operate without the advice or, as some would say, control of the Civil Service. In this case later events were to prove that such suspicions were entirely justified.

In my conversation with Selwyn Lloyd nothing was said to me about the ministerial discussions or intentions beyond a few eminently vague remarks to the effect that if no solution could be found in the near future, it would be necessary to find some way or some excuse to fight our way through the Canal. Neither on this occasion nor in the subsequent period leading up to the Suez operation was there any attempt to consult with the British representatives in the countries in the Middle East about the likely effect in their area of any action which was being contemplated, nor any warning to prepare for the local consequences of such action. The breakdown of the normal system of communications and of the normal trust between ministers and senior officials seems to demonstrate the degree of irrationality in the plans being hatched in the Government at this time. They may have had a bad conscience; they must have guessed that if any consultation took place, the response of the representatives in the field would be unanimously contrary to at least that aspect of the plans which involved apparent collaboration with Israel. Although we were told nothing by the Foreign Office, it naturally became clear from public statements and press speculation that something drastic was afoot and I and, no doubt, others felt obliged to offer some advice even though this was not solicited. I suggested in a telegram that even if action by us succeeded in restoring the situation in the Suez Canal, we should not assume that this would thereby solve all the other problems which were facing us in the Middle East. Even though the Rulers of the Persian Gulf states were fully aware of the danger to them resulting from nationalist and anti-British propaganda flowing out from Egypt, they would not automatically be able to join with us in expressing public approval or relief that action had been taken against Egypt, nor would this automatically stop the influences which were making their position and ours difficult.

The first news of the beginning of the final act of the drama, the ultimatum given by the British and French Governments to Egypt and Israel telling them that they should both withdraw from the Suez Canal and failing this, that action would be taken against them, came to me not in any message from the Foreign Office but as a report on the BBC World Service. Even if the failure to consult British representatives beforehand may be partly explained by the knowledge of ministers that they would receive responses which would be unpalatable to them, this second failure to inform us even shortly before the publication of the ultimatum could only be felt by someone in my position to be both thoughtless and irresponsible. It was a fairly hectic scramble during the next fourteen days, until the termination of the operations in Egypt and the acceptance of the United Nations intervention. We had to try to forecast what the reactions were likely to be in the Persian Gulf states and to take such precautions as were available to us which might discourage subversive acts, and be prepared to deal with them if they occurred. Meanwhile a fairly steady stream of messages were sent to London about the local reactions and conversations with the Rulers and other leading people. On 3 October, immediately following the announcement of the ultimatum, I expressed the view to London that public reaction in the Gulf would depend largely on the line taken by the Egyptian radio but it was to be expected that there would be strong reaction against the announcement of our intention to reoccupy key points on the Suez Canal and our demand that Egypt as well as Israel withdraw from it. This would be taken to mean that we were taking sides against Egypt. From the local point of view it was most important that our actions should, so far as possible, be represented as designed to stop the fighting and to secure Israeli withdrawal rather than to secure the Canal, which to the people in the Gulf would seem only to be threatened by Israel.

It is important to realise that at that time and for a considerable time thereafter there was no glimmering of understanding by us of the degree of collusion which is now known to have taken place with Israel. The nature of the ultimatum was clearly one-sided. It demanded that both Israel and Egypt should withdraw from the neighbourhood of the Canal. Israeli forces had reached nearly to the Canal by invading Egyptian territory. The Egyptians were in their own territory and defending it against external attack. It was possible to believe that we were rather clumsily taking advantage of a situation that had arisen in the course of the war between Egypt and Israel. It was unnecessary, and at that time would have seemed almost inconceivable, to think that we had had any share in promoting the situation which made this ultimatum possible. The reactions of the local people in the Gulf showed that they had fewer inhibitions. They decided from fairly early on that we were acting for the benefit of Israel even if it could not be proved at that stage that we had colluded with Israel beforehand. This is not the time nor the place to attempt even a summary of the main lines of the history of the Palestine question as it arose out of the welter of contradictory undertakings and assurances given by the British Government during the First World War. It must suffice to say that even for Arabs who were not directly affected by this question, such as those in the Persian Gulf, the creation of the State of Israel and the wars that had already taken place between it and its Arab neighbours had produced both a real revulsion on the part of virtually every inhabitant of the area against Israel and the belief that it would be suicidal for anyone to express the least doubt about the rightness of the Arab cause. Since the Suez Canal action was undertaken with the presumed purpose of maintaining or strengthening the British position in the Middle East, it is even now hard to fathom how it cannot have been clear, even without receiving opinions from the British representatives on the spot, that action taken against an Arab state which was at the time fighting against Israel could not fail to be regarded by all Arabs, even those most friendly to us, as a betrayal of our relationship with them.

I telegraphed again on 3 October to give the first reactions in Bahrain, which I said were a wide acceptance of the view that we and the French instigated the Israeli attack in order to have an excuse to reoccupy the Canal; mystification at our veto of the Security Council resolution; criticism of our association with the French, who were generally disliked only less than the Israelis and whose participation cast extra doubt on our motives; comments received even from 'reasonable' people who would not themselves necessarily share this view, that the vast majority of opinion was for Nasser right or wrong. I suggested that it was impossible that opinion in the Gulf should see the operation as other than Israeli aggression on Egypt. Our attitude would be judged according to whether it was presented as taking advantage of this aggression or designed to put an end to it. If, as was happening at present, the former impression gained ground, this would cause us more difficulty than anything else that could happen.

The Ruler of Bahrain took the situation fairly calmly. He immediately issued a prohibition on demonstrations which were not approved by his Government and told us that the Bahrain police might have to call on the assistance of British forces should they require it.

I had a conversation with the Ruler on 2 November. I told him what was going on so far as I was aware (still mainly from the BBC) and the reason for our action as described in Government statements from London. He demurred only mildly at what I had said and commented that we had got ourselves into this situation by not being firm enough early on. This was clearly intended as a reference to the situation in Bahrain. He thought that we had not given him sufficient support in taking energetic action against those members of the population who, in his view, were making unreasonable demands for participation in the government and in various other directions. Later on he sent a message asking why the British Government could not take action against Israel as well as Egypt, to make them stop fighting and drive them back over the frontier.

It is symptomatic of the lack of understanding of the real situation prevailing at that time, even in the middle reaches of the Foreign Office hierarchy, that on receipt of my telegram reporting this conversation, a minute was written in the Foreign Office saying that until we took effective action against the Israelis we should have increasing difficulties in the Persian Gulf states, even with our best friends there, the Rulers. In view of the information which has subsequently emerged about the consultation which had taken place between the British, the French and Israelis, it must have been out of the question that we should take 'effective action' against the Israelis.

The Ruler of Qatar, who was normally an easy-going old gentleman, reacted more forthrightly. He told the Political Agent on 1 November that he could not believe that the British Government had done what the broadcasts from London clearly said they had done. Other Governments might behave like that but the British Government never had in the past. It passed his understanding how they had now done so. In future he would hold that nothing was impossible. He and his people were Arabs as were the Egyptians. Arabs were united in their hatred of Jews; Jews had attacked Egyptians; the British Government must be in league with the Jews; the British Government action broke international conventions. But in spite of his strong feelings he would do everything in his power to protect the foreigners in his state. A telegram from Kuwait on 3 November said that the Shaikhs and the more responsible older Kuwaitis had remained stoutly behind us but were under increasing strain on their loyalty in face of local and external pressures. The conflict with the Egyptian army and Egyptian casualties would intensify feeling against us and the Political Agent foresaw the likelihood of deterioration in the situation there. The only thing that would alter that would be an immediate move by us to return the Israelis to their frontiers. This produced the further comment in the Foreign Office that there was no doubt that in all the Gulf states the British were believed to have acted in collusion with Israel and that up to then we had done nothing which would help to dispel that impression. I commented further on 3 November that apart from the short-term security danger, I was particularly concerned about the long-term effect. Our continued attack on Egypt while doing nothing against Israel was the one thing that might make Kuwait and perhaps Qatar think of changing their relationship with us. It was no good hoping that even the Rulers would see the Egyptians as we did. We were in fact drawing very deeply on an accumulated fund of goodwill of the Rulers. Some of this goodwill was of course interested since their own continued existence depended ultimately on our support and they must be weighing this factor with the disadvantages of acting against the emotions of the majority of their subjects. It was hard for us to claim that we were not fighting with Israel when our air attacks were in the process of destroying the Egyptian Air Force, which would otherwise be operating against Israeli forces. I said that I was taking the line that once we were established in the Canal zone, we could start securing Israeli withdrawal.

The Trucial States were less affected by the situation and the Rulers were confident of being able to keep things under control, but in Kuwait there was increasing pressure on the Ruler to boycott British commercial interests. There was particularly strong feeling among the numerous Palestinians who occupied posts in the government service there about the fate of the refugees in the Gaza Strip.

In response to these reports about the difficulties arising with opinion in Kuwait, the Department concerned in the Foreign Office suggested that the Foreign Secretary might send a letter to the Ruler. They put forward a draft which included a passage to the effect that it had been alleged that when Israel attacked Egypt they were acting by prior agreement with the British Government; the Foreign Secretary could give the Ruler of Kuwait a most solemn guarantee that there was no truth whatsoever in this suggestion. Not surprisingly, in view of later information on what had really gone on between the British and French Governments and the Israelis, the paper containing this draft was subsequently marked with the words 'Action suspended'.

The ending of the operations and the beginning of the British and French withdrawal brought about an immediate easing of the tension in Kuwait and an early end was foreseen of the boycott of British goods which had taken place.

At the same time as reporting and attempting to forecast the local reactions, we had not been idle in more practical measures to prevent, or if necessary to deal with, any trouble that might arise and threaten British interests in the Gulf. The most dramatic incidents occurred in Bahrain and necessitated the actual intervention of British forces to restore and maintain order, but the situation in Kuwait was more dangerous in that disturbances there or a policy of denying the export of oil to the United Kingdom would have been potentially more serious. The decisions for the disposition of British forces in or near the Gulf area were taken in the Local Defence Committee, Persian Gulf, which consisted of the Political Resident as chairman and the heads of the three British forces present in the Gulf. During this period the deliberations of the Committee were enormously helped by the presence of the Commander-in-Chief, East Indies, Admiral Biggs, and by occasional visits from the Head of the Royal Air Force in Aden, Air Vice-Marshal Sinclair. The forces normally available in the Gulf consisted of three naval frigates based at Bahrain, and a Royal Air Force presence at the joint civil and military airfield at Bahrain, the armament consisting of nothing more than a few transport aircraft. Owing to the previous troubles in Bahrain, there had also been a small British army presence established consisting normally of one company in Bahrain and one at Sharjah in the Trucial States. There were also the Trucial Oman Levies, a local force with British officers, the other ranks consisting of recruits from the Trucial States, which was intended to keep order and assure the frontiers of their area but whose use was in extremity contemplated for Bahrain as well. At this period of the Suez operation the forces were augmented by the presence of the cruiser HMS *Superb*. The Aden base, which contained quite large formations of British troops and aircraft, was regarded as the normal source of supply for reinforcements required in the Gulf and others could even be obtained from Kenya, where a British military presence still existed. There was no difficulty in making this chain of reinforcements operate effectively. The greatest problem was to guess the right timing at which extra forces might be required and to find acceptable accommodation for them during periods of waiting. Bahrain and Sharjah were accustomed to a British military presence and there was no particular political difficulty about increasing it in the circumstances, but with Kuwait it was quite another matter. There was no tradition of British military presence there apart from occasional friendly visits by one of the frigates and it was our clear understanding that any premature deployment of British forces north of Bahrain might have exactly the consequences which we were anxious to avoid by acting as an apparent threat and provocation. On the other hand if things went wrong, we might anticipate that there could be an urgent request from the authorities there that we should provide help and support. It was one of the many cases in which having adequate forces 'over the horizon' was clearly the right political solution, but this had extremely difficult logistical consequences for those who had to supply and look after these forces and have them available for operation at short notice. The Local Defence Committee was in almost continuous session during the early days of the Suez operation, meeting sometimes several times a day. In the apparent absence of any interest being shown from London in our situation, and in view of the obvious preoccupation of the political and military authorities there with the operations in the Canal, there was no time for, or purpose in, submitting proposals to London and waiting for approval. We did what we thought was necessary, informing London by sending telegrams announcing our decisions and deployments, in case anyone wanted to tell us that we ought to be doing something else. The clutter of communications and the lack of high level attention available for anything other than the immediate requirements of what was going on in Egypt, at the United Nations and in Washington led to the result that the most important decision which we took in Bahrain was not commented on for ten days, when a small sign of alarm was registered and we were told to modify slightly the action which we had taken, as will be described below.

The general security plan was to bring to Bahrain such troops as were necessary to provide for the safety of the oil installations and to give support to the Bahrain police in coping with the disturbances which took place in the town and, as regards Kuwait and Qatar, to have ships lying within easy reach which could be asked to come into those states and take any necessary action requested by the Political Agents if they were asked by the authorities to do this, or if the authorities appeared to be losing control of the situation. One frigate each was first sent to lie near but out of sight of Kuwait and Qatar. The Local Defence Committee was told on 31 October that this could be supplemented by HMS *Superb* carrying troops, which would be embarked at Sharjah, to the vicinity of Kuwait but also remaining out of sight, and that this position could be held for about four or five days. This was not so easy as it sounds and demanded considerable cooperation and forbearance on the part of all concerned. The climate in the Gulf even at the end of October is exceedingly hot and conditions cannot have been at all enjoyable on board a ship with a sudden increase in the complement of a large number of soldiers. On 1 November the Local Defence Committee telegraphed to the Political Agent, Kuwait, that he could call forward the naval force now standing off Kuwait to intervene if and when he thought this necessary either at the request of the Ruler or if the latter's authority had broken down. The telegram was of course repeated to London, but did not surface in the Foreign Office until 5 November, when they commented in a minute that this instruction should only have been transmitted with the Foreign Secretary's authority – but accepting that in present circumstances this would have involved dangerous delay. It seems then to have taken the Department a further seven days to find anyone to authorize a telegram to me and this was finally sent on 12 November, to the effect that intervention in Kuwait could take place only with the Foreign Secretary's authority, except in extreme emergency. I was asked to inform the Foreign Secretary if I thought that an immediate decision by the Political Agent was likely to be necessary in order to protect lives and the security of the oil installations, and I was instructed to amend the instructions to Kuwait accordingly.

I replied the next day that I did not now think it likely and that the Local Defence Committee had already proposed the withdrawal of the forces concerned to Bahrain. I added that the instructions to Kuwait had been amended to authorize the Political Agent to call forward the force in extreme emergency only.

I forbear to comment further on the state of affairs in London which this episode reveals. So far as Kuwait was concerned, it is impossible to say, even with hindsight, to what extent these preparations played a part in keeping the situation relatively quiet. One of the senior Shaikhs in Kuwait said a little later that he had been perfectly clear that the British would intervene if the situation got out of control. It must also have been well known to a number of people there that the naval dispositions had been taken, including the presence of an unusually large warship within fairly close range of Kuwait. Nothing was said about this on either side but it is probably to be concluded that the naval presence was useful in strengthening the hand of those who were working within the state to maintain order and discouraging those who might seek to upset it. This delicate balance must have been hard to understand for those who were unaccustomed to the complexities and nuances of the situation in the Gulf. The Local Defence Committee had at one point in the early days to reject firmly but politely the suggestion coming from other military authorities further away that they were prepared to offer aircraft to fly British troops directly into Kuwait as a precautionary measure.

In Bahrain, as recorded above, the situation rapidly became more overtly dramatic. A procession of protest was allowed but this got out of hand and the situation went beyond the power of the Bahrain police even though they had been considerably strengthened by the introduction of British officers and better training. The police reported that they were unable to exercise adequate control over both the main town of Manama (where the government offices were and the main commercial centre and the British Political Agency, and where the majority of foreigners lived) and Muharraq (the second largest town, joined to Manama by the famous causeway, the scene of the trouble earlier in the year and which contained the airfield and the RAF base). The slipway and marine repair installation of Gray Mackenzie, the British shipping firm which operated throughout the Gulf, was set on fire and petrol bombs were thrown. Finally the crowds approached the offices of the Adviserate and Belgrave asked me on the telephone, on behalf of the Ruler, for the intervention of British forces to help the police to control the situation. We had already received authority to use British forces in these circumstances and they came into immediate action, patrolling the external roads so as to free the police for action within the built-up areas. A curfew was ordered by the Bahrain Government. British troops were also deployed to protect the oil installations which lay at some distance from the town but at which a large number of workers were initially on strike. Some of the British people living in Manama were temporarily evacuated to accommodation at the oilfields, and those living in an exposed block of flats just outside the airfield perimeter at Muharraq had also to be moved. The causeway joining the two islands was impassable for some days. Until it was cleared, we hired a helicopter from one of the oil companies to maintain liaison between the main island and the airfield. We also tried using this machine to drop leaflets on the crowds urging them to remain peaceful. This was successfully accomplished until it was found that the bundles of leaflets were not dispersing themselves satisfactorily on their way down from the helicopter to the ground and therefore risked causing injury if they happened to hit one of the demonstrators on the head. So we had to call off that particular piece of do-it-yourself psy-war.

All this naturally led to a requirement for setting the reinforcement process in train. We began it with one of the shortest telegrams on record to Aden: 'Send Cameronians soonest'. When they had landed, they told us that they realised they were arriving at the right place when they saw a column of smoke rising from the burning shipyard on the causeway. They were soon able to clear the road through Muharraq and the causeway without casualties and to maintain the road in a usable state for the remainder of the emergency. The use of the airfield for civilian flights was suspended during this period partly in order to conserve fuel, which was in itself becoming quite a serious problem. More reinforcements had meanwhile arrived in Bahrain in case they were required to go on to Kuwait. Their presence also meant that we were amply provided with resources in Bahrain to deal with any continuing problem there, but in the next few days the situation began to improve. It was agreed that *Superb* could return to Bahrain to refuel and give the troops on board a chance to stretch their legs on dry ground for twenty-four hours and on 10 November I was able to report to the Local Defence Committee that the likelihood of our having to intervene in Kuwait was less. By the 14th it was agreed that *Superb* should finally return to Bahrain and that precautions should generally begin to be wound down. We were even able to start discussing amongst ourselves what should be the future dispositions of British forces in the Gulf and agreed that in addition to the normal naval and RAF presence, it would probably be adequate for one company of infantry to be held in Sharjah and Muharraq.

CHAPTER 9

# Turkey 1958-62

WHEN WE ARRIVED IN Turkey from Arabia, it felt as if we were coming home. There seemed to be much less of a gap between us and the Turks than between them and the Arabs. Some of my colleagues who had spent more of their time in the sophisticated metropolises of Western Europe felt they had come to the back of beyond. How could we both be right?

Part of the answer may be obtained from a brief sketch of the history and origins of modern Turkey. In the 17th century the Ottoman Empire stretched from the gates of Vienna to Baghdad, from the Crimea to the Yemen. It was a multinational empire dominated by the Ottoman Turks but allowing a certain amount of freedom for people of other religions, who were organized in communities under their religious leaders. For example a Greek Orthodox Patriarch was installed in Constantinople, as it was then called, from the time of its conquest by the Turks in 1453, and has remained ever since. After the failure of the second siege of Vienna in 1683, Ottoman power declined, sometimes gradually, sometimes in the form of large losses of territory following wars with Austria and Russia. During part of this process the martial habits of the Ottoman rulers declined to such an extent that there was a period known as the 'Tulip era' because the Sultans paid more attention to the breeding and production of tulips in their gardens than to conquering the infidels. It is even rumoured that in order to show off the beauties of their flowers more conspicuously during evening parties, they fixed candles to the backs of tortoises and had them walk to an fro through the tulips.

The diminution of the Ottoman Empire was completed during the nineteenth century as a result of wars and insurrectionary movements among the minorities in the Empire, Greeks, Rumanians,

Bulgars, Arabs etc., often supported by either the Western powers or Russia.

During all this time the Turks acquired a reputation for ruthlessness and ferocity which has to some degree clung to them ever since. This was partly because they were alien in dress, religion and habits to many of their foes, partly because they used fear as a tactic in pursuing their conquests and because their administration tended to be haphazard. Partly also, it has to be said, because violence is endemic in much of that part of the world where they operated. Can we really say with confidence that the state of affairs in Iraq and the Balkans is better now than it was when they were part of the Ottoman Empire? But the 'Terrible Turk' has become a stereotype from which it is now very difficult to move.

Controversial as it is, a word must be said about the Armenians. These are a people of unknown origin who have lived for hundreds of years in eastern Asia Minor and the southern Caucasus. They have had the misfortune to be, through most of their history, sandwiched between larger forces on either side of them. They were a border state between Rome and the Persians or Parthians, occupied sometimes by one, sometimes by the other, and sometimes independent. They were Christians from early on, but this unfortunately did not promote friendship between them and their much larger Christian neighbours, the Byzantine Greeks. Later they found themselves between the Ottoman Empire and Russia. Many thousands lived in the borderlands of Russia. Many others lived throughout Anatolia, the upland area of Turkey, and many thousands in Istanbul (formerly Constantinople). One of their other misfortunes was that in eastern Turkey they occupied areas which were also inhabited by the Kurds, a Moslem, Indo-European speaking people, just possibly descended from the Medes of biblical times. The Kurds tended to live on the hilltops and had a well-deserved reputation for brigandage. The Armenians tended to be cultivators of the more fertile parts of the country. Throughout the later part of the 19th century there were stories of oppression of the Armenians by the Turks, and of revolutionary movements by the Armenians against the Turkish Government. These stories were taken up by western opinion so that after the Congress of Berlin of 1878, which only just succeeded in preventing the complete defeat of Turkey by Russia in one of their many wars, the British Government appointed a number of vice-consuls at various points in central and eastern Turkey, whose main job was to report on the state of the Armenians in their areas. The continual nagging by the British of the Ottoman Government about their treatment of the Armenians, contrasted with indifference on the part of Germany, was a factor in the disastrous diplomatic process by which Turkey joined the wrong side in the First World War. Eastern Anatolia became the theatre for bitter hostilities between Turkey and Russia, in the course of which the Russians had no hesitation in trying to mobilize their fellow Christian Armenians to operate behind Turkish lines and act as an irregular advance force to prepare the way for Russian troops. The Turkish Government, finding that this produced unacceptable danger to their forces, ordered that the Armenian population of east Anatolia should be removed from the frontier area and resettled in Syria.

It is here that we get to the nub of the question. The Armenians and their supporters claim that there was, in the course of these events, a deliberate decision by the Ottoman Government to massacre large numbers of the Armenians. There is no doubt that many thousands died. The exact number will never be ascertained, and of course varies enormously according to who is working out the sums. The Turks would claim that conditions in eastern Anatolia, owing to the war, were in a high state of disorder and privation and great numbers of people were dying and getting killed on all sides. There is little doubt that in some cases the Kurds came down from the hills as the Armenians were making their way westwards and despoiled the passing convoys, no doubt also killing some of the Armenians. In the absence of proof of any direct order from Istanbul that the Armenians should be massacred, the best judgement is perhaps that there were sins of omission rather than commission, in other words that the Turks did not take sufficient precautions to guard the Armenians as they were moving, and that this was largely responsible for the numbers of deaths which occurred. The dispute rumbles on to this day. For a time Armenians went in for a campaign of assassination of Turkish diplomats. At the same time they have been very busy with propaganda, including, most recently, attempts to persuade the European Parliament to agree to a resolution that the present Government of Turkey should publicly apologize for the crimes of its distant predecessors as a condition of entry into the European Community. The Turkish version has largely gone by default. One might comment that there are other members of the European Community, or prospective members, who carried out atrocities of one kind or another and have not, so far as I know, been asked to submit to public breast-beating in this way. At the end of the First World War the situation in eastern Turkey, which had been unfavourable to the Turks, was transformed by the Russian Revolution, which enabled them to advance to the present-day frontiers of Turkey. In the course of doing so, they drove the Armenians before them into what became, first of all briefly, an independent state of Armenia, then the Armenian Soviet Socialist Republic in the Soviet Union, and which has now again reverted to independence.

On other fronts the Turkish armies were defeated and Turkey was threatened with disintegration by the victorious allies.

At this very time, however, emerged the extraordinary figure of Mustafa Kemal Ataturk. He was a Turkish general who had played a great part in the Turkish victory at Gallipoli. He now managed to move, either with or without the connivance of the dying Ottoman Government, to central Anatolia, where he proceeded to set up an alternative government. This gathered military and political support and moved to Ankara, the future capital. His programme for Turkey was radical in the extreme. He renounced the external possessions of the Ottoman Empire, saying that in future Turkey would be within the borders of the Turkish nation, and laid out a thorough-going system of constitutional reform. A leading element in this was the separation of religion from government. The Ottoman regime had been very much under the thumb of the Muslim divines, who in the view of many people were largely responsible for the decline of Ottoman power by their refusal to sanction innovation of any kind.

Secondly, he proposed the institution of western legal codes instead of the existing codes, which were largely religious in origin, and he proposed to abolish polygamy, sanctioned by Islam. He did not wish to legislate against people being Muslims and, contrary to general belief, he did not try to abolish the wearing of the veil by women by legislation, but only by persuasion and example. In the very early stages of the realization of this programme, Turkey was threatened by an invasion from Greece. In this she was taking advantage of the peace treaty which had been imposed on the Istanbul regime, and which gave Greece a foothold in western Anatolia, and she was backed by Lloyd George, the then British Prime Minister. The Greeks eventually extended their military offensive almost as far as Ankara, but were then massively defeated by the Turkish forces and driven into the sea at Izmir. The western powers then accepted the existence of Turkey within the national boundaries laid down by Ataturk.

In proposing this modernization of Turkish society, Ataturk was building on a tradition of reform which had begun in tentative ways in the nineteenth century, but he imposed a greatly accelerated timetable and a determination not only to talk about Turkey becoming European, as some of his predecessors had done, but to bring this about within a short span of years. Turkey was thus, by the forties and fifties, a country with a Europeanized superstructure of parliamentary Government, western education, particularly in the Universities, an increasing degree of western culture, demonstrated in the theatre, opera and ballet, superimposed on a still largely peasant state in which many of the inhabitants were poised between acceptance of the reforms and the maintenance of some of their older traditions. Some of the troubles which ensued were due not to the attempt to impose new ideas, but to Ataturk not having had time to spread these ideas into the wider and more far-off segments of the population.

From the point of view of someone arriving there for the first time, the intelligentsia had a charmingly fresh approach to western ideas and culture, often illuminating aspects of it which we had for too long taken for granted. The peasants had the virtues we like to

*Turkey v. Scotland at the Stadium in Ankara. Luckily for me Turkey won and I was cheered in consolation on leaving the ground!*

associate with a simpler way of life, such as astonishing hospitality in spite of their poverty, remarkable honesty, remarkable native common-sense and an openness to ideas which had reached them by education or tradition. I remember an episode in which we were picnicking on a hillside not far from Ankara and an elderly villager came to greet us. We happened to comment on the number of shells lying about on the surface of the hill and he proceeded to give us a short description of the geological process by which the sea had once covered the area and which accounted for the shells being there. On another occasion I visited, with Turkish friends, relatives of theirs living in a village on the way to Istanbul. While sitting down to lunch in a village house, our host cross-questioned me very acutely about the British attitude towards the European Common Market. Further south in the forested area leading down from the Anatolian plateau to the south coast, a villager complained of interference from the Government in Ankara in the way the local people should manage the forests, a subject on which they thought they knew much better than the bureaucrats. This echoed uncannily a poem written a hundred years or more earlier in which the locals are complaining about a law passed in Istanbul planning to extend its authority into the remoter areas. In this the phrase occurs: 'The law is the Sultan's. The mountains are ours'.

Another surprise – it should not have been – was the richness and diversity of Turkey's historical and archaeological past. Monuments of great interest and beauty were spread out before one both in the ancient cities and in distant archaeological sites throughout the country. The main road system was already fairly good by the time we were there, and the long drives through the Anatolian countryside, with its pastel-shaded hills and occasional fertile valleys, were particularly memorable.

There are of course defects. The Turkish authorities have long had a rather cavalier attitude to human rights, particularly as regards the treatment of prisoners, and the failure to grant cultural autonomy to the large Kurdish minority has in the end led to a running civil war in the south east which has still not been overcome. In criticizing the treatment of the Kurds, we should not forget that we have failed over I do not know how many years to pacify Northern Ireland and that this conflict too has been associated with cases of overreaction and miscarriage of justice. One of the problems has been the weakness of the Turks in public relations, partly due to inexperience, partly to an almost wilful feeling that they disapprove of the science altogether: if people want to know more about them they should come and ask. The opposite is in fact the case, the historical stereotype of the 'Terrible Turk' has to be overcome if they want to obtain the approval of the rest of the world. This means that they have to work even harder than those who do not enjoy a reputation of that kind. It is bad luck but unfortunately a fact of life.

The stereotype of Turkey has interacted with other countries in the most curious way. Turkey is probably the only country whose affairs have decisively influenced the course of two parliamentary elections in Britain. Gladstone's propaganda on the so-called Bulgarian atrocities played a major part in his electoral campaign in

1876. The British people were even said to be divided between Atrocitarians and Anti-atrocitarians. These arguments probably contributed to Gladstone's return to power in 1880.

Secondly, the confrontation between British and Turkish forces at Çanakkale in 1922, after the defeat of the Greek invasion of Anatolia, led to the break-up of the war-time coalition between Liberals and Conservatives in the British parliament and to the defeat of Lloyd George in the ensuing election. Disraeli's more favourable view of the Ottoman Empire, manifested at the Congress of Berlin in 1878, was to some extent inherited by Curzon and latter-day Conservatives, who were inclined to see the Ottoman Empire as a barrier to protect the route to and from India from the Russian threat. Nevertheless after the Congress of Berlin, at which Britain had seemed to be resisting excessive claims to Turkish territory, the British Government showed active concern for the Christian inhabitants of the Ottoman Empire, who were alleged to be suffering from oppression.

The zeal of the British to interfere in the welfare of the minorities in the Ottoman Empire was fuelled by two other rather accidental considerations. One was the prevalence of a classical education in Britain, which influenced much of the governing class, inducing it to believe that Greece was the cradle of civilization and the source of our democratic constitution. When Byron and his friends espoused the cause of Greek independence in the early 19th century, they no doubt believed that they were helping to restore the Athens of Pericles. In fact many, if not most, of the Greeks who were pursuing this aim were far more interested in resurrecting the Byzantine Empire, which was nearer to them in time and in spirit. This would not have been nearly so potent a war cry with British and western opinion, since the word 'Byzantine' had for long had a pejorative connotation as meaning excessively intricate and obscurantist, often referring to these failings being present in bureaucracy.

The other element was the love affair between Britain and the Arabs, which produced some fine literature, as for example in Doughty, Gertrude Bell and T.E. Lawrence. Some of this gave a picture of the Arab as a 'noble savage' being oppressed by the wicked

Turks, particularly of course in the more lurid passages of T.E. Lawrence, whose veracity on this question has been subject to much questioning.

Pro-Turkish writing is more scattered and less accessible. Lady Mary Wortley Montague, the wife of the British Ambassador in the early 18th century, called attention even at this early date to the double standards by which Turkey is so often judged. In a letter of 1718 she writes, apropos of reports of the vandalization of one of the monuments in the Hippodrome, that those who report this 'took the report from the Greeks who resist with incredible fortitude the conviction of their own eyes whenever they have invented lies to the dishonour of their enemies'. Later in the same letter, she says, 'You will object that (in Turkey) men buy women with a view to vice. In my opinion they are bought and sold as publicly and more infamously in all our great cities'. Aubrey Herbert wrote charmingly and with genuine affection for Turkey before the First World War, but his writings did not make so much impact as those of the Arabists. The French writer Pierre Loti is better known for his novels about the sensual, not to say sexual, adventures of his autobiographical hero with ladies escaping from the harem than he is for the impassioned defence of Turkey, which he wrote later during the Balkan Wars.

The Liberal preoccupation with alleged Turkish wickedness was to some extent inherited by the Labour Party. I remember years ago at a lunch party given by the Foreign Secretary for a visiting group of Turkish provincial governors, a Labour member of Parliament who had been invited to take part entered the room announcing in a loud voice, 'I am a Phil-hellene'. Fortunately, I think none of the Turkish visitors knew what on earth he was talking about. He was no doubt thinking of his image with his Greek Cypriot constituents in North London, but it was a curious way to start a conversation with Turkish guests.

Finally on this subject, it is a curious quirk of history that Ataturk received no credit with Liberal opinion for having overthrown a despotic regime and installing parliamentary government with western codes of law. One might have expected that he would get the same applause as 19th-century liberators and reformers like Bolivar, Kossuth, Mazzini, Garibaldi and others.

Another matter over which the Turks are much criticized is the question of Cyprus. This island has for hundreds of years been inhabited by a large population of people of Greek descent and a smaller population of people of Turkish descent. I was associated in 1959-60 with the concluding phases of the negotiation which led to the establishment of Cyprus as an independent country with a constitution that set up a federal system of government, with a Greek President and a Turkish Vice-President, and an assembly in which the numbers were proportionate to the numbers of the two kinds of inhabitants. Only a few years after these agreements were made, the Greeks were mainly responsible for sabotaging the proportionate nature of the administration and carrying out what later became known as ethnic cleansing in parts of the countryside. It became only too apparent that there were elements on the Greek side who saw the agreement merely as a stepping stone towards union with Greece, and matters were brought to a head when a nominee of the Junta of Colonels in Greece took over the Presidency by a violent coup against Archbishop Makarios, who had made the agreements, with the obvious intention of speeding up this process. The Turks not unnaturally felt it necessary to intervene militarily to protect their community in 1974, and the island has remained divided ever since. The Turks probably hold a somewhat larger share than would be strictly justified by the proportionate numbers of the population. On the other hand, since their intervention, there have been practically no instances of civil strife or terrorist attempts on life, in contrast to the state of affairs just before this.

We arrived in Ankara near the beginning of the winter in 1958. I had been advised that it would make a good impression if we arrived in a Turkish ship, which we did. There was, and probably still is, a line of Turkish passenger ships plying between southern Europe and the western and northern coasts of Turkey. We embarked at Naples and had a very comfortable voyage. The Captain very obligingly put up a Union flag on his yardarm as a compliment to our presence aboard. On the way we stopped for an hour or two at Athens and were received at the British Embassy. I claim to be the only person who has visited Athens and not seen the Parthenon. My colleague insisted on spending almost all the time of our visit talking about the Cyprus question, which was then in one of its final throes before being resolved by agreements some months later. So my wife went sightseeing while I stayed cloistered in his study.

The Embassy at Çankaya is on the hill that rises to the south of Ankara above Kavaklidere. Ataturk lived at the top of the hill and this continued as the Presidential Palace. Legend has it that the site of the British Embassy was chosen on the same hill, just below the President's Palace, because it was thought that the water supply would be more reliable since it was using the same pipes that went to the President's Palace. In my experience this was not always borne out in practice, but there was the very convenient arrangement that when we ran out of water, we would call on the fire brigade to come with a tanker, the contents of which they pumped up into the cistern. Luckily we did not have to rely on this source for drinking water, which arrived in demi-johns from an unknown spring and which was reputed, naturally, to be the very best available. Among the many estimable characteristics of the Turks, one is that they are connoisseurs of water and usually good providers of it. I remember driving in eastern Anatolia in the summer. Having stopped at a roadside fountain, we drank thankfully from the water which poured out of it, confident that it would not only be comparatively pure but also of a delicious quality. (It is a characteristic shared with the Spaniards. When later on we were travelling in southern Spain and filled our water containers at a roadside fountain in the middle of Granada, opposite the Alhambra, a taxi driver drove up on the same errand and we asked whether the water was good. He replied without shadow of a doubt, 'El mejor del mundo' – the best in the world).

The Embassy building has a complex history. The first building there was what later became the Chancery. It was originally intended as the Ambassador's residence, with a small office facility. After the Second World War, the present residence was built next to the original building, which then became entirely devoted to the offices.

The very large garden was on a steep slope continuing well below the Embassy buildings down to the floor of the valley. In the late 50's there was not very much building beyond the Embassy garden. In fact there were rumours that not long before, wolves had been seen in the garden in a particularly harsh winter. Even in the late 50's and early 60's there was still abundant wildlife. I spent several happy half hours armed with binoculars watching a Hobby hawk nesting in a tall tree at the bottom of the garden and a Scops owl made its monotonous call from a poplar tree outside our bedroom window.

The garden was under the control of Cemil, a wonderful gardener who had been instructed in his task by one of our predecessors, Lady Kelly. Like most gardeners, he was intensely conservative and when we delicately suggested some alteration or innovation in the varieties of flowers which he grew, he would almost always reply that he did not think Lady Kelly would have approved and that, more often than not, was the end of the matter.

The most noteworthy event which took place in the garden in our time was the production of Milton's masque, *Comus*. We were fortunate to have in Ankara at that time a Covent Garden producer who was taking part in the work of the Turkish Ballet and a very gifted Head of the British Council, and they collaborated in this production, in which they were able to persuade the two Kenters, Yildiz and Muşvik, to participate. Yildiz, dressed ravishingly, all in white, was the Lady and sat surrounded by the children of the National Opera School. Muşvik was Comus, who appeared dramatically on the top terrace of the garden and swooped down with arms outstretched almost appearing to fly until he arrived at the stage at ground level and tried unsuccessfully to ensnare the Lady. The Kenters, being of partly English descent, were willing and able to give perfect expression in English to Milton's verse and one can only say that the whole setting must have rivalled that at Ludlow Castle, where Comus was first produced.

The Embassy guest lists of the time might make interesting reading. Lord Mountbatten dropped in for a Cento meeting. The Duke of Gloucester paid a visit in interesting circumstances. He was President of the War Graves Commission and paid the first visit by anyone in this position to the War Cemeteries of the British and Anzac forces at Gallipoli. He arrived in the Royal Yacht *Britannia* and I went to meet him at Çanakkale. We spent the day driving and walking around the cemeteries which were kept by the Commission. We then steamed up to Istanbul, where the Duke disembarked in order to pay a visit to the Turkish President, General Gürsel, in Ankara – most appropriately since the General had as a young man served in the Gallipoli campaign. However, even their best friends would not say that either the General or the Duke were fluent conversationalists. After the exchange of a few remarks about Gallipoli, the conversation was somewhat laboured and the Turkish Foreign Minister, Selim Sarper, and I, who were acting as interpreters, had to extrapolate rather wildly on the remarks of our principals in order to keep matters going. It is a curiosity of history that the Gallipoli campaign, so full of bitter memories for the British, Australian and New Zealand troops who took part, was regarded on both sides as an unusually gentlemanly campaign – some would even say, perhaps, the last gentlemanly campaign. The memories of it were celebrated in a friendly manner by the participants of both sides and even in my time, a few elderly British, Australian and New Zealand veterans made the pilgrimage to Turkey to join with their former opponents in remembering the battles of long ago. And so, although rather exhausting for the interpreters, the meeting passed off well.

Another pleasant occasion was the visit by Sir Alec Douglas-Home, then Foreign Secretary, on the occasion, I think, of a NATO meeting. In the course of this I remember him talking after dinner in the Embassy with a Turkish politician, making comparisons of the amount of acreage which was needed by a sheep in the highlands of Anatolia or in the borders of Scotland.

One of our most notable visitors was Dame Ninette de Valois, who, by extraordinary chance, had agreed some years earlier to found a classical ballet company in Turkey. This ambitious project was coming to fruition during our time, and Dame Ninette made the Embassy her base during several visits, culminating in the first public performance. It was, I think, *Coppelia*, and was received with rapturous applause.

The capital of Turkey had been moved in the 1920's from Istanbul to Ankara. The old Embassy at Istanbul still existed and part of it was used as the Consulate-General, but at that time a suite of rooms was reserved for the use of the Ambassador, the tradition being that we should spend two or three months there during the summer. This was done on the basis that members of the Turkish Government also preferred to spend the summer in Istanbul rather than Ankara, but by my time the tradition was growing a bit thin and I had to travel back to Ankara almost every week to conduct business with the Turkish Government. The Istanbul Embassy had been built about 1850, partly under the direction of Barry, who also designed the Houses of Parliament and some of the London clubs. It bore an uncanny resemblance to the Reform Club in Pall Mall. There were also the remains of a former summer Embassy, which lay in a large park on the edge of the Bosphorus some miles north of Istanbul. Here the Embassy had been accustomed to reside during the summer at the time when the capital was in Istanbul. This summer building was burned down in 1913 and never rebuilt, but the garden was still there and provided an outstandingly beautiful place to visit for picnics etc. We once gave an open-air dinner party there under the trees for the two Ottoman princesses then resident in Istanbul, appropriately, since it was one of their ancestors who had given the site to the British in years past.

Our stay at Istanbul in 1959 was enlivened by an unusual visit. I received a message from the Foreign Office to say that Winston Churchill, by then some years retired from active politics, would like to visit Istanbul and meet the Turkish Prime Minister, Adnan Menderes. This was fine, but the context of the journey was a little more problematical. Sir Winston would be travelling on board the yacht of Mr Onassis, a wealthy Greek ship owner, as he was in the habit of doing in the summer, and I was asked to invite the Prime Minister and the Foreign Minister (Zorlu) to lunch on board the yacht just outside the Bosphorus. Although relations between Turkey and Greece were at that time comparatively friendly, following on the agreements about the independence of Cyprus, it was not an ideal mode of transport for a world statesman to use in visiting Turkey.

Nevertheless Mr Menderes took the proposal with very good grace and he and Zorlu and I made our way by launch to the yacht. The luncheon passed very well. Some of the time Churchill was wrapped in his own thoughts but there were flashes of brilliance when the conversation interested him and the Turkish Ministers were well pleased with the meeting. As well they might be, for apart from Churchill, the company was intriguing. The other passengers besides Churchill and his wife were the charming and beautiful Mrs Onassis, whom Onassis was to divorce a year later, and Maria Callas, with whom Onassis had, or was about to have, what was politely called a relationship. But the underlying tension did not show itself at the lunch table.

Menderes and Zorlu left after lunch and the yacht moved in to take up its station in the Bosphorus in front of the Dolmabahçe Palace. Churchill had indicated that he wanted to see some of the historic sites of Istanbul and I had therefore arranged for the Embassy's Rolls Royce to be waiting for us at the quay-side. But it turned out that this was not the method of transport which he preferred. Onassis carried on board the yacht a small white two-seater car which he drove himself and which was duly lifted from the yacht's deck on to the quayside by the yacht's own tackle. Churchill then descended the gangway and mounted the passenger seat of this car with Onassis driving. I followed in the Rolls. There was also the necessary clutch of security vehicles trailing behind. It turned out after a short time that Onassis, although born in Turkey, did not know his way about Istanbul. So I stopped the cortege and mounted the small seat at the back of Onassis' car, into which I could barely fit, but which gave me a better chance of directing him on the way to go. The Rolls followed empty in case of any unforeseen emergencies. We duly visited Aya Sofya, the Blue Mosque, the Hippodrome and looked from the outside into the Topkapi. Churchill did not want to get out and have a closer look, but declared himself well satisfied with the excursion and congratulated me on my knowledge of the topography, though I am not quite sure how much of my running commentary on the history of the city he was able to take in. We returned to the quayside without further incident and returned on board the yacht, where I had been invited to stay for supper.

While waiting for the meal to be prepared, I found myself standing at the yacht's rail with Onassis, looking at the sordid beauty of the Istanbul water-front in the gathering dusk. Turkey was at that time passing through one of its economic crises and I asked Onassis, to fill in the conversation, what he would do to restore the situation. 'Quite easy,' he replied, 'I would bring in ten thousand Greeks'. I did not pass this advice on to my Turkish friends.

Later in the year political storm clouds began to gather, leading eventually to the dramatic and tragic events of 1960/61. These events demand a rather fuller treatment, which I will attempt to give, accompanied by another small excursion into recent Turkish history which is necessary for an understanding of them.

The story really began in 1950, when the first multi-party election resulted in a very large majority of seats in the Grand National Assembly being won by the Democrat Party led by Menderes. Owing to the electoral system, the size of the majority exaggerated the difference in the numbers of votes. The DP won an even larger number of votes in 1954, but in 1957 they had gone down to 47% with the Opposition PRP getting over 40%.

According to the Government, the Opposition Party (the Peoples Republican Party) spent most of these years trying by extra-parliamentary means to overthrow the result of these elections. According to the Opposition, the Government used increasingly unconstitutional means to suppress the activity of the Opposition. In May 1960 the Government was overthrown by a military coup, and after a lengthy trial, the Prime Minister, the Minister for Foreign Affairs and the Minister of Finance were hanged and other members of the Government and of the Democrat Party were condemned to varying periods of imprisonment. By the middle of 1962 Parliamentary Government had been restored. What I have to say on this period is derived largely from the despatches and other papers which I sent from the British Embassy to the Foreign Office and on personal memories. It is by no means a comprehensive history.

A curious thing happened about my reports. In 1990/91 when they became publicly available in the Public Record Office (as most official papers do after thirty years), lengthy extracts were printed in Turkish in one of the leading daily papers in Istanbul. I do not know whether to take this as a tribute to my reporting or as an indication of the poverty of Turkish reports on the subject, even thirty years on.

It has to be remembered that a genuine two-party system was a comparative novelty in Turkish political life. Moreover, the 1950 result was more than a change of government. It was the end of an era. The PRP saw itself as the inheritor and successor of Ataturk, and therefore as having a right to govern and to apply the principles of secularism and etatism. There was some tacit recognition of the fact that the Ataturk Revolution had not altogether succeeded in spreading itself into the countryside. The support for the PRP tended to be provided by the educated classes, the Civil Service and the larger towns. The Halkevis (peoples' houses) were intended to provide political education for the masses of the peasantry and thus to complete the spreading of the revolutionary beliefs into areas where this had not been done by Ataturk himself But in many parts of the country the rule of the PRP was felt as an attempt by the centre to impose rules on the countryside, where these had not previously been applied. So it was inevitable that the first serious and well-organized opposition party, the Democrat Party, should seek its political support in areas where the PRP had not penetrated, or by its excessive penetration, had made itself unpopular. This included, but was by no means wholly limited to, the question of religion.

The phrase 'fundamentalist secularism' has only recently been coined to represent the attitudes of the intellectual Ataturkist elites of the first Republican period. There is no doubt that the description had a modicum of truth, and that a resurgence of religious influences was seen as one of the greatest dangers to which Ataturkist Turkey was exposed. This again made it inevitable that an opposition party would find it hard to resist, even if it wanted to, the temptation to show some acquaintance with, and sympathy for, the still predominantly Moslem culture which provided the mainstay of village life. This element did not become a major factor in the political scene until fairly late in the life of the Menderes Government, but the financial help for the building of mosques was a symptom of the hostility of the two parties towards each other.

With three successive defeats, frustration rose in the Opposition, and since nothing could be achieved in Parliament with its vast Government majority, the temptation became irresistible to use non-Parliamentary means. In this context it became of importance that most of the press and of the academic elite were hostile to the Government. This gradually led to attempts by the Government to suppress the more vigorous expression of criticism by the suspension of newspapers and, in one or two cases, by the imprisonment of journalists. At the same time, and perhaps because of the difficulty of expressing criticism through the press, the Opposition Party undertook fairly frequent political excursions into areas outside Ankara and Istanbul for the purpose of holding political meetings and rallies. Inönü, the leader of the PRP, took part in several of these excursions and his great and continuing prestige in the country led the Democrat Party to be particularly sensitive to his participation. These meetings or attempted meetings sometimes led to scenes of public disorder and eventually to attempts by the Democrat Party to prevent their taking place. On one or two occasions, when it seemed necessary to involve units of the army in maintaining order or in preventing Inönü and other Opposition leaders from attending meetings in the provinces, there was the first manifestation of what eventually led to the overthrow of the Government: namely the reluctance of the army to be involved in actions which seemed to be due more to politics than to a genuine breakdown of security. In particular the army was reluctant to take part in actions designed to stop Inönü, whose career as Ataturk's principal general was still vividly remembered, from taking part in political manifestations. Looking back, it is incredible that the Government did not take warning from this situation.

The continuing resentment of the Government at the attacks on them in the press, and the activity of the Opposition in staging well publicized political meetings throughout the country, eventually led to their using their large majority in parliament to set up a committee of investigation into the activities of the Opposition. This was composed entirely of Democrat members of the Assembly. It was gradually given exceedingly large powers in its own right, as well as the function of reporting back to the parliament, and these in the end included the power to limit or suppress political activity, and even to restrain publication of debates in the parliament relating to the activities of the commission.

What turned out to be the fatal element, which was added to this generally tense atmosphere, was the decision of students in Ankara and Istanbul to take to the streets in protest against the suppression of the press and of political freedom. The police were unable to maintain order effectively in the face of these protests. The Government seemed to see themselves faced with the alternatives of either calling a new election a year or two before it would normally have been required, or of imposing ever more severe repressive rules on political expression either in the press or by demonstration.

The curious and tragic fact is that in the view of most observers at the time, the Government would very likely have won an election if they had called it in the spring of 1960. They still had widespread support in the countryside, owing to the programme of economic development which they had carried out and which was proving of benefit to at least some areas of the country which had previously been neglected. The question was seriously debated within the Government, but in the end they decided that they could not take the risk of calling an election. Part of the reason for this decision must lie in the development of the character of Menderes. He had started as a more or less conventional populist politician, determined to maintain the movement of Turkey towards Western standards of prosperity and political life, and particularly to spread these benefits to the areas of the country, notably in rural districts, which had not previously benefited from them. Hence the rather extensive programme of building roads and of infrastructure programmes such as the construction of hydro-electric installations in country districts, a new oil refinery in the south-east and the attempt to improve the productivity of agriculture by the encouragement of mechanization both on the ground and in the construction of silos to handle grain exports. These were supposed to result from the agricultural development programme (but in fact, in many years they were used to handle imports of grain which became necessary owing to bad harvests and the rapid expansion of the population). This development programme was undertaken without very much regard to the dictates of overall planning or financial rectitude, and to a large extent thanks to financial help from the West and Western financial institutions.

I had some personal experience of this programme when I had to be present at the inauguration of installations in which British firms were involved. One was the oil refinery at Mersin, financed by a consortium of oil companies including British ones. To me, not yet well acquainted with the force of traditional observances in the life of modern Turkey, the most startling feature was that when the foundation stone was laid by the Prime Minister, a sheep was sacrificed on the spot and its blood mingled with the mortar with which the stone was secured. Another, perhaps more reflecting the rather chaotic nature of some of this programme, was when I participated in the inauguration of a hydro-electric dam at Hirfanli, in a remote district not far from Ankara in the Anatolian countryside, for which a British company had supplied the generating plant. I was invited to be present at the ceremony with the leading members of the Turkish Government and to say a few words to celebrate the British participation. It was a cold winter's day with snow falling, when we wended our way along country roads, I in the official Rolls Royce, wondering when it was going to scrape its bottom on the ruts, until we reached a desolate hillside where the dam had been constructed, and where for the ceremony rows of seats had been provided for the visitors from the surrounding area. They had been persuaded or cajoled to come and watch. They seemed to be more interested in the prospect of a free meal than in that of greater supplies of electricity resulting from the dam, and there was some very audible murmuring when the food-stuffs seemed to be delayed en route. After the Government spokesmen had made their orations, the time was approaching when I would have to add my words, which I had carefully written out in Turkish, when the public address system broke down. As it seemed impossible to repair it, I soon found myself standing in the snow storm shouting in my rather elementary Turkish about the delight of the British to be able to participate in this development, to an audience of Anatolian peasants who were much more interested in the prospect of lunch than in hearing anything that I or anybody else was going to say to them.

Through these and similar experiences Menderes began to see himself as having a special role in the future development of Turkey, to believe that this role was unique to him, and that he ought not to take the risk of his being supplanted in power by anyone else, who would not be able to carry it out so successfully. This attitude was unfortunately exaggerated out of all knowledge by a set of circumstances of a purely accidental nature. During this period the negotiations on the future of Cyprus had been conducted sometimes with acrimony, but in the latter stages with considerable goodwill on all sides and eventual success. As one of the later stages of this process, the Turkish Prime Minister and senior Ministers were invited to London to take part in a final set of negotiations with the Greek Government and the two communities in Cyprus. On the flight to London in an aircraft of Turkish Airways, the aircraft ran into fog shortly before it was due to land at Gatwick and crashed. There were a number of fatal casualties, but Menderes and other members of his Government and staff survived. This led Menderes and a number of his more fanatical supporters to claim that his survival had been secured by divine intervention and that this reinforced the unique position which he held in Turkish life. That position was, by implication, held to be not susceptible to the normal rules of political behaviour in a democracy. The popular acceptance of some such view, though no doubt to quite a large extent politically organized, was demonstrated on the return of Menderes to Turkey, when on his way from the airport into Istanbul a large number of sheep, goats and camels were sacrificed as his convoy passed, with the implication that almost divine honours were being attributed to him.

Another important motive in the reluctance of the Government to call an early election was undoubtedly their anxiety that, if they were to lose, their activities over the past two or three years would be exposed to severe and hostile scrutiny by an incoming Government of the PRP, and the realization that these activities, and probably some of the financial dealings in which they had taken part, would not redound to their credit, to put it mildly. As I reported at the time, the Government lost its head at the thought of losing power and hastened that event by the unwise measures which it took to prevent it.

The other extraordinary misjudgement which overtook them towards the end of their time was the apparent belief that the measures which they were undertaking against the Opposition could be carried out by political means, or solely with the help of the notoriously inefficient police force, and would not require the participation of the army in the maintenance of public order. Alternatively, if this were to be required, they believed that the army would in the end obey the Government rather than follow their preference for the person of Inönü and the ideology which pervaded the officer corps, and which was deeply hostile to the flirtation of the Government with Islam. It very soon became clear in practice how fallacious this judgement was. The student demonstrations increased in frequency and intensity. The police were incapable of maintaining order except by the use of violence; the army were called in and quickly showed their extreme reluctance to be involved, and on several occasions manifested their sympathy with the demonstrating students. It did not help the DP that millions of the inhabitants of Anatolia supported them. These people were not on the streets of the capital cities and could not be transported there. The abuse of parliamentary majority had transferred the struggle to the streets, where the Opposition held the majority. It is important to note this cooperation, which in many other countries would be unexpected, between the students and academic staff and the officers of the army. One of the reasons was that the army had been seen by Ataturk as in the last resort the mainstay of the revolution which he had accomplished, and the military readily saw themselves in that role. In a longer historical perspective, it may also be recalled that under the

Ottoman Sultanate the only two institutions of higher learning which were permitted were the War College and the Faculty of Political Science. This arose from the perceived need to produce officers and government servants who were adequate to handle the modern apparatus of a state. For it was already becoming clear by the end of the 19th century that Turkey had to become progressive in this sense in order to maintain its position in the world. The 1960 revolutionary movement leading to the coup was to quite a large extent created in the Faculty of Political Science, and took its effect because the products of the War College were unwilling to suppress principles in which they also believed. A conspiratorial movement began among middle-ranking officers of all three services. General Gürsel, the Army Commander, agreed to join, but was prepared to support revolution only as the very last resort. He made his position very clear, however, in a paper which he sent to the Minister of Defence, deploring the use of troops against students, calling for the resignation of the President and the abolition of the Parliamentary Commission. He went on leave from his post in early May, shortly before the coup, and agreed to become the leader of the new regime as soon as it took place. The Chief of Staff of the armed services, General Erdelhun, appeared to be entirely out of touch with the feelings of these officers, or to misjudge their importance, and remained personally loyal to Menderes.

The actual conspiracy was made between a fairly small number of colonels and majors, and equivalents in the other two services, and the coup itself was carried out very largely by officer students from the War Colleges in Ankara and Istanbul, who took over the centres of power in the two cities, as well as the radio stations. My first knowledge of what was happening came when I received a telephone call very early in the morning from the security guard at our offices next to the Embassy Residence, which was very close to the Presidential Palace on the hill of Çankaya. The guard told me that he could see from within our compound that the Presidential Palace was surrounded by tanks. I asked him which way the guns were pointing and he said inwards. This made it clear what was happening and I think my report to London for once out-paced the earliest news reports which were sent by journalists. The coup was immediately successful and virtually bloodless. There was no significant opposition by other sections of the armed forces and only minor opposition from certain elements of the police force.

The President and all the members of the Government and of the Democrat Party in parliament were put under arrest, as well as the Chief of the General Staff of the armed forces and some other administrative and military personnel. The Committee of National Union, composed of the principal officers who had carried out the coup, set themselves up as the government of the country under the leadership of General Gürsel. One of their first tasks was obviously to decide what to do with the politicians and others whom they had taken into custody. There was, in fact, practically no acceptable alternative to the course which they decided to pursue, namely to put them on trial. It should be remembered that this coup took place only two years after the revolution in Iraq. This had caused widespread execration abroad owing to the bloodthirsty nature of the action taken against the members of the Royal Family and leaders of the previous Government. On the other hand, it was clearly felt to be unsafe for the future of the revolutionary movement that they should be banished to remote parts of Turkey, or allowed to seek refuge abroad. Moreover, the Turks are a naturally legalistic people. The proceedings of the Government, Parliament and Administration were governed by a detailed constitution and laws resulting from it, and the main charge against the former Government was that it had infringed not only the spirit of parliamentary democracy but also specific guarantees of parliamentary and press freedom. There were, no doubt, elements in the armed forces from the beginning, as there were at the end of the process, who were determined that the ultimate penalty should be imposed on at least some of the members of the previous Government, but they seemed to have been persuaded that Turkey's aspirations to westernness, which they were in fact protecting by their action against an allegedly unconstitutional regime, would be better served by legal process; probably also with the expectation that this might result in some of the ultimate penalties which they advocated. So the trials were instituted, held before a special court sitting in the island of Yassiada, and lasted for the best part of a year. No doubt many learned volumes have been written on the conduct of these trials from a judicial point of view, of which I am unaware. I can only give an outsider's impression based on reports from observers from the British Consulate at Istanbul who were present for most of the time. The impression was that the trials were conducted with a mixture of fairness and partiality. They appeared to be taking place in a general framework in which there was no doubt that crimes had been committed against the Constitution and other laws, and that the main duty of the court was to apportion the blame for this among the defendants and to pass the appropriate sentences. Initially a great deal of time was wasted on charges that seemed to have little relevance to the essence of the situation and to the guilt or innocence of the accused, and it was impossible to resist the deduction that some of these had been put forward largely with the intention of discrediting the members of the Government in the eyes not so much of the judges as of the people outside. It was as if there was a general attempt to 'demystify' the position, particularly of Menderes himself. There were criticisms of some of the technical features of the conduct of the trials, particularly the limited facilities for the accused to confer with their lawyers and the acceptance of evidence that in a British court at least, would have been regarded as hearsay and therefore not acceptable. On the other hand, the accused were given the possibility of making long speeches in their own defence.

It was not until 1961 that the court entered on the really important aspects of the charges, the unconstitutional behaviour of the Government and parliamentary majority in setting up the Commission of Investigation, and giving it powers which seemed to infringe parliamentary liberties and various particular provisions of the Constitution. At this point there emerged, with the utmost clarity, the question that was to preoccupy opinion in Turkey and outside for a considerable time to come, namely the question of the death penalty being imposed on some of the accused. The Constitution of the Turkish Republic provided for this penalty to be imposed to punish breaches of the Constitution and accordingly the prosecution asked for the death penalty to be imposed on a large number of the Government who had been involved in attempts to suppress the Opposition during the previous two or three years. It was this element in the whole story which chiefly preoccupied opinion in western Europe and the United States. In order fully to understand the reasons for this, it is necessary now to look back at the conduct of foreign, as opposed to domestic, affairs by the Menderes Government. Turkey had been firmly aligned with the west ever since the ending of the Second World War. From 1947 onwards the 'Truman Doctrine' extended American support to Turkey against the pressure which it was then experiencing from the Soviet Union with regard to the Straits and Eastern Turkey. This was confirmed and generalized by Turkey's entry into NATO in the early 1950's. Subsequently Turkey played a leading part in the formation of the Baghdad Pact between Turkey, Iraq, Iran, Pakistan and the United Kingdom with American backing, which represented a deliberate attempt by the Menderes Government to extend to parts of the Middle East the western system of security from which Turkey itself benefited. Moreover there followed an initial period of great difficulty over the Cyprus question in the middle 50's, in which the Turkish government appeared intransigent and almost certainly organized the anti-Greek riots in Istanbul in 1956 (as was brought out at the Yassiada trials). The final conclusion of the Zurich and London agreements, setting up the independence of Cyprus with a division of power between the Greek and Turkish communities, represented a statesmanlike compromise which restored relations with Greece. Membership of the western organizations gave frequent opportunities for meetings between Menderes and Zorlu on the one hand, and European and American statesmen on the other, who formed a favourable view of the importance of Turkey to the alliances and of the robust conduct of foreign affairs by the Menderes Government. There was therefore a strong tendency in western circles to regard the leading members of the Turkish Government as statesmen who had conducted the affairs of their country in a manner that responded to the needs of the very difficult times in which they lived and in full accord with the Governments of the west with whom they were allied and associated, and with many of whom they had satisfactory personal relationships.

This may be the place to attempt a brief assessment of the character of Menderes and of Zorlu. (Polatkan, the Finance Minister, was smaller fry, with whom I was personally almost unacquainted.) I have already described the deterioration in Menderes which power produced and, as power became more absolute, he became more reckless in its use both in dealing with the Opposition and in a massively underfinanced development programme. However, this should not obscure his basic commitment to the good of Turkey as he saw it, which was a more powerful motive than any idea of personal aggrandisement.

Zorlu was, in my opinion, an extremely good Foreign Minister. He spent his earlier years in the Foreign Service, and was therefore well equipped as a technician. He added to this a personal drive and determination which sometimes took on a buccaneering quality. He saw Turkey's interest as being closely associated with the west. He was sometimes unscrupulous in his methods of achieving this aim, and in his efforts to get the best advantage from it for Turkey. His weakness was his lack of a political base in the country. This deprived him of the quality of management and compromise inseparable from the character of a politician, and led him into extreme positions in internal affairs, in which he was not expert.

Returning to the question of death sentences, the reactions of western countries naturally reflected their own political traditions. The judicial execution of political leaders for crimes against the state had been out of fashion for a long time in the west (with one exception) – in France for nearly two hundred years, and in England for more than three hundred. The exception was, of course, the Nüremberg Trials following on the Second World War, at which an international court decreed the execution of German leaders who had carried out crimes against humanity. This would have been regarded as not providing a precedent for the execution of national leaders by national courts, nor did the apparent or alleged offences of Menderes and his Government appear to be on anything approaching the same scale as those of the accused at Nüremberg. In Turkey, on the other hand, execution for political offences had been carried out much more recently. The executions of some of those who resisted the imposition of the Ataturk reforms in Eastern Turkey, for example, could well have been in the living memory of people who were still alive in 1960. There was thus ample opportunity for collision between western opinion and the hard men of the armed forces in Turkey. Much time and effort was spent by western governments in seeking means of influencing events in Turkey with regard to death sentences on members of the previous Government without giving too blatant an appearance of intervention in the internal affairs of another State. It was recognized by many of us, including from the beginning the British Government, that it might well be counter-productive if there were too publicized action by western governments or representatives to try to influence the result of the trials. On the whole, therefore, the preferred action was to furnish Ambassadors in Ankara with authority beforehand to take steps at the moment they judged appropriate by letting selected people in the Turkish government know of the likely reactions in the west if death sentences were carried out, but without seeking publicity for this action. The timing was, of course, very crucial, since it would almost certainly produce a bad effect if it could be represented that the western governments were seeking to influence the course of the trials. On the other hand it was widely believed, as turned out to be the case, that there might be an extremely short interval between the imposition of death sentences by the court and the carrying out of some or all of these by the authorities. Accordingly the action generally taken was to let the Turkish Foreign Minister, Selim Sarper, know in advance that we had instructions on these lines and to seek his co-operation in passing this knowledge on to President Gürsel and leaving it to them to decide how much if at all, and at what stage, the views of the western governments should be made known to other members of the Committee of National Union.

In return Selim Sarper made known to the Ambassadors who carried out instructions on these lines that both he personally and, he fully believed, General Gürsel, were in favour of any death sentences being commuted to imprisonment and as the trials progressed

*Greeting the Shah of Iran at Ankara airport, 1961. Front row: US Ambassador, the author, The Shah, General Gürsel, President of Turkey.*

towards their conclusion, we were told that on the best calculations they could make, it seemed likely that a majority of the Committee of National Union would be of the same opinion. Matters were by no means helped, however, when an American News Agency published a story more or less to the above effect, saying that Gürsel and Sarper were in favour of clemency. In the end the court passed death sentences on some twenty of the accused, including President Bayar, Menderes, Zorlu, Polatkan, and a number of other deputies and members of the parliamentary Democrat Party. Most of these verdicts were not unanimous but passed by a majority of the judges; the only ones which were unanimous were the four above mentioned, namely the President and the three leading ministers. The exact sequence of events following these sentences and the course of discussion within the Committee of National Union are not fully known to me. The widely accepted version is that while there probably was still a majority in favour of commuting the death sentences, the Committee was also fully aware that there was a strong movement among a further and more shadowy group of officers who were determined that some death sentences should be carried out and who were threatening to take action on their own, even to the point of going to the prison on Yassiada and carrying them out themselves if this were not done judicially. In another even more melodramatic version, one or more officers appeared with drawn guns in the course of the deliberations of the Committee and enforced their view by actual threats. However this may be, the upshot was that the death sentence on Bayar was commuted on account of his age, but those in the three other cases in which the verdicts had been unanimous, namely Menderes, Zorlu and Polatkan, were confirmed and these people were hanged within forty-eight hours.

The reasons for the unanimous verdicts need to be considered for a moment. The cases of Bayar and Menderes were fairly self-evident. If anyone was responsible for infringing the Constitution, which carried an automatic death penalty, it clearly must have been the responsibility of these two. There was in fact some feeling that the moving spirit had often been Bayar, but with the role of the President supposed to be in the background, the executive responsibility had to rest with the Prime Minister. The inclusion of Zorlu was justified largely on the basis that he was recorded in their Cabinet Minutes as having advocated more bluntly than other people the use of non-parliamentary methods of controlling or suppressing the Opposition. But in fact in his case and in that of the Finance Minister, it was generally believed that a large part of the reason lay in the reputation for corruption which these two suffered from to an almost universally recognized and detested extent. I have no evidence to prove or disprove this allegation, and the fact that it was so generally believed seems to have been enough to influence the judges, even though corruption in itself did not specifically call for a death penalty. A wonderfully sardonic comment was made on this situation by Inönü, the Opposition leader. He said to a friend, 'How lucky it was that we, the Turks, are not Christians. There is Jesus Christ and the two thieves.'

The executions produced almost as little reaction in the West as they did within Turkey. The exception, unfortunately for me, was that on the news being received, the Government in London put out a statement to the effect that while this was a matter of Turkish law, nevertheless the British Government regretted that it should have been found necessary to invoke the death penalty. The British Government took steps some weeks previously to make clear to the Turkish Government the 'strong feelings which would be aroused in the UK by the imposition of death sentences'. This provoked a very severe reaction from the Turkish Government and I was lectured by the Foreign Minister, who was personally incensed at this 'holier than thou' attitude on the part of a friendly government, when, as he said, he and others had risked their necks trying to prevent these executions taking place and had very nearly succeeded. The impression was given that but for the friendly feelings which were felt towards me, we were not far from a withdrawal of Ambassadors, which in diplomatic parlance is the next step towards breaking off relations. However, this storm blew over almost as quickly as it had arisen.

This may be the moment to comment on a more general aspect of the diplomatic reaction to a change of government brought about by violence, as occurred in Turkey. I, in common with other western representatives, had, of course, done my best in the preceding period to become personally well acquainted with the members of the previous Government in the furtherance of our task of maintaining, and if possible improving, relations between our countries. We may have held the view that they were pursuing an unwise and possibly unconstitutional course in the actions that they were taking in regard to the Opposition. Nevertheless our business was with the Turkish Government while that existed. Then, following the coup, and the recognition of the new regime by our Governments, we had to appear to forget previous acquaintances and friendships, and to get on as good terms as possible with the people who were then governing Turkey. *Raison d'état* predominated and personal feelings had to be forgotten. It was lucky that ethical foreign policy had not yet been invented. There was a particular case of conscience with regard to one of the conspirators, who had been the Commander of the President's Guard. He had clearly felt it necessary to put his allegiance to the State and the constitution above any allegiance to the person of the existing President, and we had to accept that the new Government endorsed this view. It was perhaps historically comforting to recall that the same thing had happened in this area in the past, when the Pretorian Guard made and unmade Roman Emperors, and janissaries had done the same for Sultans. The importance, from the British national point of view, of making friends with the new regime, whatever its origin, was demonstrated in 1961, when I had to obtain, with considerable difficulty, the authority of the Turkish Government for British aircraft to overfly Turkey on their way to support Kuwait, with whom we had a defensive alliance, on the occasion of an earlier Iraqi threat to invade that country. I had been able to explain this situation generally to one of the members of the Committee who was at dinner at our Embassy a night or two earlier, and had received his comment that it was a good thing to support one's friends. I have every reason to think that this conversation was of some value in obtaining the consent of the Turkish Government when the moment came, even though they were initially highly doubtful as to whether they would give us this concession.

While the drama of the trials and sentences was taking place, equally important events in the long-term were being pursued at Ankara, where a Commission had been set up to draft a new constitution for the Republic, one which would be designed to prevent abuses of the kind which were alleged to have happened under the Menderes Government. This was done by a committee largely composed of academics and approved by the Assembly, which had been selected rather than elected by the military government. It was put to a referendum which technically approved (6 million yes, 4+ million no, 2.4 million abstained). Its adoption was followed fairly soon by parliamentary elections which gave a majority to the People's Republican Party, and led to İnönü becoming Prime Minister. The former supporters of the Democrat Party largely followed the new Party which had been set up, the Justice Party, since it was forbidden to use the name of Democrat Party. The constitution was full of checks and balances designed to limit the power of the Executive. It was the feeling of some people, probably justified by hindsight, that it was in some respects an over-correction, and went too far in making it difficult to exercise effective government in Turkey and particularly in denying the Executive the power to call elections when the parliamentary situation became an obstacle to government and administration. Some of these points were corrected in the 1981 constitution.

Meanwhile the other Ministers and some of the Parliamentary deputies of the Democrat Party remained for varying lengths of time in prison. My wife had cakes baked in the Embassy kitchen and sent them by devious means to our friends who were in prison to supplement their regulation diet. This must have been well known to the Turkish authorities but they never raised any objection. The politicians were gradually released and finally a symbolic conclusion was brought to the whole affair about ten years ago when official ceremonies of rehabilitation of Menderes and his colleagues took place at the National Memorial at Ankara. There may well have been elements of political calculation in this action, but the fact that it could take place without apparent opposition, and with at least the tacit acquiescence of the armed forces, gives evidence of political maturity. There have been various ups and downs in the democratic process in Turkey. Perhaps the best general verdict was given by Bülent Ecevit, the present (November 2000) Prime Minister in the course of a talk which he gave while in opposition to the Royal Institute of International Affairs in London under my chairmanship. When he was questioned about the outlook for democracy in Turkey, he replied that, given all the upsets which the democratic process had received, the situation seemed to suggest that democracy was very strong in Turkey, in view of the fact that it could survive all these changes and still maintain its position as the basic principle of political life, even though not always perfectly applied. He is now leader of a Coalition Government and Turkey has been accepted as a candidate for entry into the European Union. This in my view would be an appropriate step to symbolize the ultimate success of

*Princess Alexandra arriving at Istanbul airport, c.1961.
Ines on her right, Rupert greeting her.*

Turkey's decision to become a democratic Europeanized country. There are various hurdles to be overcome, such as the Armenian lobby in France and the point of view of Greece, though there has been a remarkable outbreak of amity between the two countries following the earthquakes that they each suffered recently. One of the most difficult of such hurdles has been the reluctance of Germany to be seen to be opening its frontiers to a further wave of immigration of Turkish workers, of whom nearly two million are already present in that country. Human rights, Cyprus and the Kurds are put forward as obstacles by those who have an inbuilt reluctance to accept the possibility of Turkey changing its historical stereotype. None of these is insuperable but will require immense effort on the part of Turkey's Governments and constructive sympathy on the part of the existing members of the Union.

It was with great regret that we moved from Turkey to London in 1962. After my retirement, we returned many times either as tourists to see parts of the country that we had not been able to visit earlier, or in my capacity as Chairman of the British Institute of Archaeology in Ankara, which has a fifty-year long experience of contributing to the unravelling of Turkey's very rich archaeological heritage. One of the most notable of our journeys was when we drove from England to Ankara and then continued, with the help and support of the Turkish authorities, to visit the extreme east of the country. We explored Erzerum, with its wonderful Selçuk monuments and its tangled history of Russian and Turkish wars. Then we continued past Lake Van to Kars, where we stayed with the Provincial Governor in the government building built by the Russians when they were in possession of this city. Then finally to Ani, situated a few hundred yards from the Russian frontier on the banks of a gorge which separates the two countries. This was the first place occupied by the Selçuk Turks in their advance into Asia Minor and contains an extraordinary mixture of Armenian and Selçuk architecture, some of it still well preserved after a thousand years. Having had a good look at the monuments, we were then entertained at luncheon, after which two folk singers gave an extempore performance commenting on our visit, followed by a stunning display of Turkish folk-dancing.

CHAPTER 10

# London 1962-66

I WAS APPOINTED ONE OF THE Deputy Under-Secretaries at the Foreign Office, a group of about half a dozen, each supervising a geographical area or a function. Above us was the Permanent Under-Secretary or head of the office. My area was the liaison with the Ministry of Defence and the Chiefs of Staff and with the Intelligence Departments. A good deal has been written since that time about the functioning of the Intelligence Services. I do not propose to add to this. I strongly disapprove of the accounts which have been written, and of the weakness of the enforcement mechanism in preventing this. In addition to the Official Secrets Act covering all members of the Government Services, those connected with the Intelligence Services had to make a more cogent undertaking not to reveal anything relating to their work, and this was imposed for an indefinite period, i.e. not just for the period they were carrying out this work. I am old-fashioned enough to believe that such undertakings should be honoured.

My work in connection with the Chiefs of Staff meant that I sat with them for part of their deliberations and could be called on to give political advice, or at any rate to report to the Foreign Office and return with such advice on the next occasion. We prided ourselves on this long-standing arrangement, by which a politico-military view could be obtained, believing that this fairly elementary method of ensuring co-operation was not enjoyed to the same extent by most other countries.

These years were a period of considerable turbulence in internal politics in the United Kingdom, with Macmillan retiring as Prime Minister in 1962, followed by the fall of the Conservative Government in 1964. The Cold War reached its climax with the Cuban missile crisis in 1962, but most of this took place, literally as well as figuratively, in the stratosphere and after it had been overcome, foreign affairs were somewhat calmer than in the immediately preceding years. We had Foreign Secretaries about as different in character and calibre as it would be possible to imagine in the persons of Alec Home and George Brown. I had experience of the latter also in my next post after 1966. It was a good training in the skill claimed by the British Civil Service of working impartially for whatever Ministers were in power, though it must be admitted that in some cases it is more difficult to carry out this task with conviction than in others.

During these years I had two foreign excursions of some interest. One was to Washington to make contact with the American Intelligence Community, with whom we maintained particularly close relations. In the course of this I was asked by a young lady at a party in the Embassy whether I was 'M' (the abbreviation given to the Head of the Secret Service in the James Bond books). I replied that if I was I would not tell her, would I, and with that she seemed to be satisfied. At a small dinner kindly given for me by the Secretary of State I was able to recall in reply to the toast that when I had sat for the entrance examination into the Foreign Office I had been asked by one of the Interviewing Board why I wanted to join the Foreign Service. I replied that I wanted to know how things really went on. Now that I had at last become acquainted with the Intelligence Community, my wishes were to be fulfilled.

The other journey was to Aden, where there was an insurrection taking place which was causing quite serious trouble to the British Forces, and Duncan Sandys, Minister of Defence, went to see for himself what was happening and asked me to go along to have a look at the Intelligence set-up. Not long into the flight we were told by the pilot that he had received a message containing a report that a bomb had been placed on our aircraft. We all managed to look very brave and said we would prefer to continue the flight to Libya, where we were going to make a fuelling stop, rather than return to London. After a thorough search at El Adem, nothing was found on the aircraft and we continued successfully to Aden (this was before the time of Colonel Qaddafi).

There were two other much-valued privileges: one was that in the absence of the Permanent Under-Secretary, I had on more than one occasion the duty of attending on the Queen when she received incoming foreign Ambassadors who presented their credentials to her on taking up their posts. The other was that the Lawn Tennis Association, in gratitude for the services which Embassies rendered them abroad, had the pleasant habit of allotting to us two seats in the Royal Box on the centre court at Wimbledon during the tournaments and these occasionally fell to my lot.

Towards the end of this period we got into one of the many defence reviews, in which the attempt was made to match our diminished military capability to the commitments which we still had or were likely to incur. The basic problem was that in the way of resources, we were no longer a world power, but we still had the tradition that we should be able to intervene anywhere, either if a far-flung British possession was in trouble or if some humanitarian mission was required. There were various causes for this mis-match of resources and commitments. We had fought two world wars which we could not afford and which had brought us no tangible rewards. Our industrial productivity continually lagged behind that of our competitors. There was disillusion with military adventures after Suez. Nemesis occurred some years later in the Falklands. Governments were apparently unable to find the political will either to build the aircraft carriers which were necessary for the defence of the islands, or to hand over our 'kith 'n kin' to the tender mercies of the Argentines. The operation itself was of course glorious, but the risk was probably greater than that of any other operation we had undertaken.

CHAPTER 11

# Nato 1966-70

I WAS APPOINTED British Permanent Representative on the Nato Council. The title needs to be explained. The Council met at two levels. Two or three times a year the Foreign Ministers or Defence Ministers, or sometimes both, attended meetings. In between times the Council consisted of the 'Permanent Representatives', with the rank of Ambassador, from each of the fifteen participating countries, presided over by a Secretary General, who in my time was the Italian Statesman Manlio Brosio.

When I joined, the organization was situated in Paris, where it remained for the best part of a year until we moved to Brussels. The Military Headquarters of the Alliance was also situated near Paris and moved at the same time as we did, to Mons in Belgium. These moves provide a peg on which to explain the French position with regard to NATO. They had joined the Alliance on its formation. It was in fact a development of an Anglo-French Treaty concluded shortly after the end of the Second World War to guard against a resurgent Germany. However, on the breakdown of four-power government in Germany, the emphasis shifted to the threat posed by the Soviet Union and the entry of the United States into the Alliance confirmed this objective. In the early sixties the French insisted on forming their own nuclear deterrent force, separate from the joint Anglo-American nuclear forces which had hitherto been the backbone of the Alliance. In 1966 De Gaulle paid a successful visit to the Soviet Union. This made some people think that he was aiming to conduct independent relations with that country, which would not have been exactly in the spirit of NATO. In the same year he requested the removal from France of the Alliance Headquarters and the Council decided to move at the same time. Several things are not clear about these developments. Was De Gaulle motivated by his

*CENTO meeting, 1961. Left to right: Sir Roger Stevens, HM Ambassador in Iran, the author, Michael Weir (behind – later Ambassador in Egypt), Sir Harold Caccia, Permanent Under-Secretary at the Foreign Office, Lord Mountbatten, Chief of Defence Staff.*

tentative rapprochement with the Soviet Union or simply by the desire to repay the grudges which had accumulated during his time in England during the war, when both England and America failed to give him the support which he thought he deserved? Did he hope or did he expect that by banishing the military headquarters from France, he would thereby induce a dissolution of the Alliance which might improve his position in any future dealings with the Soviet Union? These are speculative questions to which clear answers may never be available.

The moves took place without too many problems and both the Council and the military headquarters established themselves in Belgium. The only major change was that the French withdrew from the military headquarters and laid down that the participation of their forces in any future NATO operation would depend on a

*NATO meeting c.1969, with Michael Stewart, Foreign Secretary.*

decision taken by the French Government at the time. Meanwhile they were unwilling, in principle, to participate in the planning for such possible future operations. In practice the split was not as great as it might have sounded. The French continued to sit as full members in the Council of NATO, although not in the Military Committee. Liaison between the NATO Command and the French forces was maintained through various devices and it became possible to discuss what the French forces would do in the event of a decision being taken by the French Government that they should participate.

If one looked at the small print of the obligations of the other members to the Alliance, the difference in the French position seemed even smaller. Each member state had the right and the duty to decide to commit its forces to the Alliance in the event of military operations being decided. There was no standing NATO command over the forces of other countries in peacetime (except for two very small Naval forces which practised together continually), so to some extent it was a case of gesture politics. This did not prevent the French representative taking an active part in the deliberations of the Council and those appointed were usually of the high calibre which one would expect from the French Foreign Service. There was, and possibly still is, a tradition that when one is at a post abroad one writes an annual report for the benefit of the Foreign Office on the diplomatic colleagues in the same post. I remember writing a generally eulogistic report on one of my French colleagues and concluding with the words, 'It is such a pity we are not on the same side'. Years earlier there was a similarly equivocal report by the French Foreign Office on a British Ambassador in Paris, of which the first four words were accidentally seen by a member of his staff. The words were '*Malgré son air idiot...*' It has for a long time been a matter of intense regret to me that relations between us and France have so seldom been cordial, in spite of the name given to the Entente formed early in the last century. One would think, looking at the map and at a lot of the history, that our interests would be similar. Territorially we both derived from the Greco-Roman tradition, with local mixtures. The French nowadays are not much more Catholic than we are Anglican. But history has pitted us against each other to a ridiculous extent, and how far back that history unfortunately runs! The wife of a colleague of mine once asked the wife of a very prominent French Minister why it was that it seemed so difficult for our two countries to be in agreement. The reply was: 'It is very simple. It was of course the Hundred Years War'. I sometimes wish history was not taught in schools. At least we ought to have text books which are agreed between traditional foes. On the Hundred Years War I prefer the formulation by a delightful young school teacher which I heard while she was showing a party of tourists, largely English, over one of the castles in the Dordogne. She said it was absurd to suggest that this was a war between the English and the French. It was, on the contrary, a war between two rival French dynasties, one of whom happened also to own England. On the other hand, I have recently heard a well educated Frenchman say that he found it hard to understand why the British had not been willing to accept being part of a Europe united under Napoleon, which would, after all, only have been a precursor of what we are now enjoying as the European Community. It should hardly surprise us that the original M. Chauvin was French, and indeed one of Napoleon's veterans.

Churchill's dramatic offer of common citizenship between England and France made in 1940 at the moment of the disintegration of the French Government, failed because circumstances were too heavily against it. Bringing De Gaulle to England to carry on the War was brilliant at the time, but did not cure long-standing suspicions and jealousy. Now, however, that we and France are both members of the European Community, which involves some degree of pooling of sovereignty, the degree being a matter of acute controversy, it could be thought that we could forget our historical differences and rejoice together in the new partnership. France, however, understandably, has paid much more attention to its relations with Germany than with England, and has proposed a higher degree of integration than is widely acceptable in England, in order to tie Germany more closely into the union with a view to excluding the possibility of its future independent action.

If one remains optimistic, as I am, that this absurd antagonism of stereotypes between us and the French will some time come to an end, perhaps one might feel that the name-calling between Ministers at the Hague Conference in November 2000 will oblige those in authority to take more seriously the need to rebuild confidence and friendship.

To return to NATO. This was my only experience of multilateral diplomacy, and I found it most enjoyable. There was a fruitful sense of collegiality between the fifteen Permanent Representatives, a greater freedom of confidence and communication between them than is normal between diplomatic colleagues, and a healthy tendency on occasion to gang up against our governments when we felt they were mistaken.

One of the interesting events of this period was the assumption by NATO of a role in the détente and disarmament process. It may sound odd that an organization created for purposes of defence should also deal with this subject. The initiative was due to the approach of the 20th anniversary of the foundation of NATO, by which time, the Treaty said, it would be possible for anyone who wished to do so to secede from the Alliance. There was, so far as I know, no real risk that this would happen but it was put to the rest of us by Belgium that it would make it easier for the smaller members to maintain the favourable feelings in their public opinion if NATO's purposes could be broadened to include attempts to bring about a reduction of armaments and the gradual reduction in the asperities of the Cold War. This was known, after the Belgian Foreign Minister, as the Harmel plan. The text was worked out in a late night session in my office between representatives of Belgium and the United States as well as ourselves, and successfully presented to the Council the following day. I am not sure whether we achieved any important breakthrough in the questions of disarmament, but it was certainly a gain to the standing of the Alliance that it adopted these objectives as well as military planning for defence.

The other novel development was that we set up an informal grouping of the European members of NATO known as the Euro-Group. It should be remembered that this was the period during which the United Kingdom was trying unsuccessfully to join the European Community (some sixteen years after it had been invited to do so at the Community's inception, at which time it had rejected the invitation). The proposal was put forward by Denis Healey, then Minister of Defence, at a dinner party in my house. Our motives were firstly to improve efficiency by seeing whether we could rationalize some of the supporting elements of the defence forces of the European countries such as air transport and various branches of logistics.

Secondly to give a chance of discussion among the European members of important matters which were due to come before the full Council to see whether we could arrive at a joint European view, which might have more influence than the views of individual states. Finally it was sought to keep the European idea running in a way that included the UK pending the successful conclusion of negotiations for our entry into the Community. The group met informally and carried out some useful if rather pedestrian work in the co-ordination of medical services and other such matters. It was viewed with sympathy by the United States, no doubt in the hope that its formation might eventually lead to the contribution of greater resources by the European countries to the common needs of defence. Its chief interest today lies perhaps in the fact that it was thought up for the same general purposes as the European Rapid Reaction Force which is now under discussion, sometimes of a highly controversial kind. We never got so far as that in the sixties but we shared one principle in common with the British view of the present proposals, namely that the European initiative should not be designed in any way to weaken NATO or to set up anything in contradiction to it, but rather to strengthen its purposes by the added identification of roles the Europeans might take on, in which American participation was not necessarily essential. It is perhaps curious to recall Denis Healey's primary role in putting forward the Euro-Group initiative, in contrast to the attitude he has publicly adopted to its putative successor, the Rapid Reaction Force, today.

A good deal of our time was taken up in the meetings of the Nuclear Planning Group, which consisted of a limited number of members of the Alliance, some of whom took it in turns to participate. It always included the Americans and ourselves as nuclear powers. It did not, however, include the French, who declined to submit their nuclear policy to international discussion. One of the purposes of the discussions was to establish guide-lines for the possible use of tactical nuclear weapons, that is to say those which might be used on the battlefield rather than being dropped on enemy cities. The discussions were often abstruse, but enlightened by the often very high level of individual debate between Denis Healey and his American opposite number, McNamara.

One of the joys of NATO was that alternate meetings of the Ministers took place in the fifteen member countries in turn, the other meetings taking place at the Brussels headquarters. This programme included a meeting in Iceland, which I might well not otherwise have visited. On the way the aeroplane had to be slightly diverted in order that the then Foreign Secretary, Michael Stewart, could observe from the air some of the important sites recorded in the Icelandic sagas, of which he was a serious scholar. In our spare time at the meeting we took advantage of the natural hot water supplied by the volcanic nature of Iceland's geology to have a swim in a warm water outdoor pool, and we visited the site in the countryside just outside Reykjavik where the first parliament had met, claimed to be the oldest parliament in the world. The Nuclear Planning Group also met in various countries – on one occasion, when the Italians were hosts, in Venice. Of course Denis Healey could not resist commenting in his opening remarks on the suitability of meeting at the site of the book and film *Death in Venice*.

When the organization moved from Paris to Brussels, our French friends condoled with us for having to move to '*Une ville de province*', but in fact we were very hospitably received by the Belgians and enjoyed living among them for three years. When we were due to move there, we had of course all to find places to live in Brussels. We were lucky enough to be able to rent a very fine Art Nouveau house whose garden ran back to the Bois. While remodelling the garden of this house with the help of a Flemish speaking garden contractor, I was able to appreciate the universality of Latin as the botanical

*NATO Nuclear Planning Group meeting in Venice, c.1969. Breakfast on the Grand Canal. Photograph by Denis Healey, Defence Secretary, signed on reverse, 'Pro memoria Veneziae'.*

language by exchanging names of plants with him without difficulty. One could not, in Brussels, escape the pervasiveness of another linguistic quirk. The town was officially bilingual between French and Flemish, but this did not always satisfy the fanatics on either side, who sometimes went through bouts of crossing out the directions on sign posts in the language of which they did not approve. On one occasion they went further than this. Following De Gaulle's visit to Canada in which he declared '*Québec Français*', Flamands in Brussels spray-painted a bridge with the words '*Kanada vlams*'. Belgium was a storehouse of Flemish paintings and of notable moderns such as Magritte and Delvaux and it had the advantage of being next door to Holland, where we frequently went at weekends to enjoy the paintings there.

The 20th anniversary of the Alliance in 1969 was celebrated by an allied naval review at Portsmouth to which the Permanent Members of the Council were invited. We flew to Southampton, transferred to a helicopter that took us into Portsmouth dockyard, thence went by launch to *Britannia*, where we accompanied The Queen as she carried out the review. As we progressed up and down the lines of allied warships and were entertained to a sumptuous lunch, I could not help recalling the very different circumstances of our yachting adventures at the 1936 review recounted above.

CHAPTER 12

# Retirement?

WE LEFT BRUSSELS IN JULY 1970 on my retirement from the Foreign Service, having attained the age of sixty. This is the age at which all government servants have to retire, except in very exceptional circumstances. The age limit was fixed when the Civil Service was first set up in an organized way back in the 19th Century. It seems to have escaped the notice of those in authority that since then the expectation of life has considerably increased, so that sixty is now an age at which many people are at least as capable as they were ten years earlier, and in some case probably more so with the benefit of longer experience. Some time after I retired I had a letter published in *The Times* saying that if the Government wished to save money on pensions a simple way to do so would be to extend the age of retirement from the Civil Service by, say, five years. There was absolutely no response. The usual answer to this argument is that if the age was extended in this way it would cause a riot among those who were expecting preferment and would have to see their hopes postponed. To counter this, it would of course be perfectly possible to make the change gradually, extending the age one year at a time. Many other European Foreign Services have an age limit of sixty-five and in some cases seventy.

I found the moment of retirement traumatic. One day you are in correspondence with the higher reaches of government and taking part in decision-making. The next day nobody wants to hear from you again. Admittedly you get a nice pension, but the sudden separation from the corridors of power is painful. Some countries ease the transition by giving retiring officers temporary posts as consultants or such like. But we do not. The argument is that if you do not see the daily circulation of telegrams etc. from abroad, you cannot know what the situation really is; therefore your advice is

*'White tie and decorations'.*

valueless. Looking back, I rather wish I had pursued a half-formed idea of promoting an association of former Ambassadors, who might meet occasionally, and sometimes have a discussion with a Minister or Senior Official in which they might possibly be able to contribute something useful from their combined experiences. Instead, I made various attempts to find alternative employment in the academic world. But in the end, perhaps fortunately, without success. However I accepted an offer which came through a series of coincidences and which coloured a lot of my efforts for the next several years. The offer was to take part in a study of a European Defence Organization within NATO and it came to me from a small research organization known as the Federal Trust for Education and Research. This was an offshoot of, and part successor to, the movement for Federal Union which started just before the Second World War both in the United States and, coincidentally, in England. I had first come across this idea by reading the book *Union Now* by Clarence Streit while sitting on the beach in Alexandria in 1938. I had been so impressed by it that I thought for a brief time of leaving the Foreign Service to return to England and take part in this movement. The core of the proposal was to form a Federal Union of the Democracies on either side of the Atlantic as a means of preventing the war which was already menacing. It was based on a critique of the nation-state as having led to most of the recent wars. It proposed a merging of sovereignty between those of them who were qualified by their democratic forms of government to join a movement that would be able to promote this cause more effectively than individual nations could. By extraordinary chance, or perhaps because the *Zeitgeist* was leaning that way, a group of three young men, one of whom was a close school friend of mine, started at almost exactly the same time to promote very similar ideas in England. These led to the formation of the organization called Federal Union. It attracted considerable support in the period immediately preceding the outbreak of war, and for the initial period of the war itself. Once the war started seriously, the protagonists of the movement were dispersed or had more immediate tasks in hand or, as in the case of my friend Derek Rawnsley, were killed in the war. The movement was revived after the war by a band of enthusiasts who recognized that it could no longer hope for early success as a political movement, but could more usefully inaugurate a series of studies on the question of Federation. This, it was hoped, would lead to a more general longer-term understanding of its advantages The inauguration of the European Community, for which Federal Union could perhaps claim some intellectual ancestry, naturally gave a sharper focus to the study of the subject of integration between countries, and the work of the Federal Trust then concentrated largely on the study of various options for the future development of the Community, with a strongly integrationist bias.

A smaller branch of the Federal Union preferred instead to deal with the wider but more distant possibilities of World Federation. I was asked to join because of my work on promoting the Euro-Group in NATO. But it was a curious chain of linkages that brought me back, after over thirty years, to promoting the ideas which had so intrigued me before the War. I joined Christopher Irwin, then Deputy Director of the Trust, in writing a book on Western European Defence and a few years later became Director of the trust. We organised conferences and seminars in various places all round the country, usually at universities, at which we assembled people from all political parties to talk about aspects of the European idea.

I was then asked to set up a branch of the European movement in East Hampshire, where I lived, with a view to achieving a favourable answer in the referendum which the Government decided to hold in 1974 about the continued membership by Britain of the European Community. It is curious to recall that on that occasion the Conservative and Liberal Parties were in favour of membership and Labour largely against. There was a general belief that Mr Wilson had called the referendum because he did not wish to take the responsibility on his own for continuing a policy that might not be endorsed by large numbers of his followers. We had a vigorous campaign, sticking posters on various unauthorized sites around the district, including railway bridges and telephone kiosks, and taking loud-speaker equipment to market places to canvas our point of view. Reception varied. I remember in one particularly isolationist stronghold I said to a recalcitrant old lady that even if she did not approve, she ought to think of the good it would do to her children, to which I got the chilling reply: 'What have my children ever done for me?' We were outstandingly successful. The referendum obtained a favourable response, our district showing the second best result in the country. We also wrote and edited various publications in which we tried to emulate the 'Federalist Papers' which had been published in the early days of the American Republic, and which had largely contributed to the formation of the United States as a federation with the constitution which has survived until today.

Do I think the same today? In principle, yes, but as a long-term goal. In my view one of the mistakes of recent European developments has been the rapid timetables imposed largely by M. Delors, the former President of the European Commission, for reaching various stages of integration. The word 'Federal' has become a term of abuse in England, differing in this from all other continental countries, although we have in our time imposed or encouraged Federal systems in many parts of the world, e.g. Canada, Australia, Malaysia, India and Germany. Moreover, they have on the whole been successful. But many people in this country still cannot accept the idea of Britain itself taking part in a Federation of European States, largely because the word has come to mean, in the popular mind, centralization rather than, as it should properly be understood, the taking of decisions at the lowest possible level so that people can feel more intimately associated with them, leaving only a few subjects to be dealt with from the centre.

Another sphere of activities was Turkey. It was the only one of the places where we had served where we returned frequently after retirement. Getting there overland was in those days quite interesting in itself. We had one gorgeous stopping place at the Bromowski castle in Carinthia, just north of the Yugoslav border. After that we tried to go by different routes through Yugoslavia, which was then peaceful under Tito's rule, unlike its present condition. One road took us through Dubrovnik with its wonderful urban architecture. On another occasion we were more adventurous and drove down the coast as far as Kotor, then up a series of hairpin bends to the old capital of Montenegro, Cetinje, where we hoped to stay, but were put off by the colour of the sheets in the hotel. So we drove on and decided to sleep in the car in a big lay-by on the top of a mountain. It turned out that this was quite near the frontier with Albania and in the middle of the night a detachment of the Yugoslav army came there on a night exercise and parked their trucks all round us. They may have been surprised to see a car with Turkish number plates (this must have been while I was still at the Embassy) so near their frontier, but they made no objection and departed after a couple of hours. We continued down the mountain to where we got breakfast at Titograd, and then on to lake Ohrid, with wonderful painted churches. Skopje was dramatic, with its mosques giving a foretaste of the east and people rushing up to us when they saw the Turkish number plates to address us in that language. How sadly different it must all be now. In London I was Chairman for about ten years each of the Anglo-Turkish Society and the British Institute of Archaeology in Ankara. The latter gave us the excuse to visit the excavations where British scholars were working. One was relevant to a controversy of today, on a site which was about to be submerged by the rising waters of a dam on the River Euphrates. The archaeologists told us that there was one advantage in working in such a situation. When they had thoroughly examined and recorded a layer of civilization on the mound, they did not have to restore it or leave it in situ because the water was going to cover it in any case. So they pushed it down into the valley and got on with the next layer. I have little sympathy with the agitation which is going on as I write (November 2000) about the effects on archaeology and the inhabitants of building a larger dam further down the river. Much of the Roman town of Zeugma will not be affected by the rising water, contrary to what is often stated in the press. The building of dams everywhere, including in this country, leads to some of the inhabitants having to be moved. This is terrible for them but in the case of the Turkish project it is going to make life far better for an incomparably larger number of people who now live in very difficult conditions in the surrounding area. I also undertook some writing and lecturing about Turkey's wish to enter the European Community, which I still warmly advocate, though it can hardly occur for a number of years.

There were many other trips to France, Italy, Spain and Germany, usually with a theme: Baroque churches in Germany, Romanesque in France, the Emperor Frederick II in Apulia and the classical sites of Paestum, Pompeii, Herculaneum on the return journey up the west coast, the Moors in Spain and so on. Home during all this time was a small farm in East Hampshire, and then a converted farmhouse in West Sussex. Small-scale absentee farming became unprofitable and the emphasis switched to gardening, to which we devoted many happy hours. I was the plantsman, pushing at the boundaries of what was possible to grow, succumbing to the charm

*Handing out prizes at flower show,
East Dean Horticultural Society, c.1990*

of the half-hardy perennials which became so fashionable with the opening of a South African supply. My wife was the colourist, often asking in despair where I was going to put the latest exotic rarity that I had acquired. Then there were the gardens to visit in Cornwall and in Wales and also those two jewels of English gardening history in the Midlands, at Hidcote and Kiftsgate. And I added to my list of Chairmanships that of the local Horticultural Society.

A curious activity in which I took part about 1980 was the publication of a book called *The Third World War*. This originated from discussions between General Sir John Hackett and the publishers Sidgwick and Jackson about a possible book of decisive battles in world history. One or other of them then had the bright idea that instead of this there should be a book forecasting a hopefully imaginary new world war to take place during the 80's between NATO and the Soviet Union. To accomplish this, Shan Hackett assembled a group of friends, mainly from the Armed Services but including also myself and a member of the staff of the *Economist.* He and I had met on various occasions in the Middle East and elsewhere. During the early years of the War he was a member of the Trans-Jordan Frontier Force and ended his military career as Commander-in-Chief of the British Army of the Rhine and Northern Army Group.

My job in the writing programme was to contribute the political scenario by which a war might have broken out, and then after its successful conclusion, to provide another scenario for the break-up of the Soviet Union and the aftermath. The greater part of the book was to be taken up by detailed descriptions of the campaign, in which the Generals, Admirals and Air Marshals could enjoy themselves describing the battles which they never actually had the chance to fight. I had just to get them in and then get them out. Planning meetings took place in the appropriate surroundings of rather bibulous lunches at the Cavalry Club.

With the Cold War still at its height, it was not too difficult to think of scenarios which might precipitate actual conflict. The ending of the story required a good deal more invention as to what might go on inside governing circles in the Soviet Union when their attack was, by a narrow margin, held somewhere near the French frontier and they had to recognize that they were not going to be able, by ordinary military means, to progress further. This included the delicate question of whether or not nuclear weapons should be used. Clearly we could not have a full-scale nuclear exchange, or none of us would have been there to write about it. On the other hand, it was difficult to think that a hard-line military party in the Soviet Union would not insist on at least a demonstration strike in the hope that this would be enough to produce a settlement favourable to themselves. So we compromised on a single nuclear strike by the Soviet Union on Birmingham, followed almost immediately by a counter-attack consisting of a single Allied strike on Minsk. This happily led to the overthrow of the Soviet Government by a conspiracy led by Ukrainian plotters and the break-up of the Soviet Union into its component parts. The latter hypothesis was quite largely inspired by the brilliant book of a French lady futurologist, *L'Empire Éclaté*, which described the strains already visible within the Soviet Union and the decline in the proportionate weight of the Russian element as opposed to those of the subject states, largely Moslem.

The book was a phenomenal publishing success, achieving entry in various best-seller lists. There was even a rumour that the American President kept a copy by his bedside. In the light of this, the publishers, needless to say, could not resist asking for some more of the same and we published a second volume called *The Untold Story*, containing various bits that had been left out of the original book. They then had what no doubt seemed an even brighter idea and asked us to do a version in which NATO lost instead of winning. Rather against our better judgement, I think, we accepted this proposal and added a story of this kind as an alternative ending to the second book. I had to describe the sort of terms that might be imposed on a defeated Britain by the Russians. I also shamelessly borrowed an idea from a book of H.H. Munro (Saki) from before the First World War, in which he similarly envisaged the possibility of a British defeat by the Germans in what he already foresaw as the coming 1914 war, and in which he described how the British Monarchy and Government escaped to India and set themselves up there as the centre of a new British Empire. In our case we provided that British Naval Forces should receive orders shortly before the cessation of hostilities that on the announcement of an armistice, they were all immediately to leave British ports and make their way to the ports of the Commonwealth countries, taking with them members of the Royal Family, who would then become heads of state of those countries. In this way they would provide for a continuation of British governments in Commonwealth countries supported by units of the British and Commonwealth Navy Forces.

*Gardening at Durford Wood, 2000.*

These would join with the United States in preventing the further spread of Russian control over the world.

Apart from these activities, I at last had time for two intellectual pursuits which had been hovering in my mind for a long time: psychical research and humanism. My interest in the former had, I suppose, begun when staying as a child in a ghost-ridden house in Scotland and was encouraged by my philosophy tutor at Oxford, who organised a visit to us by J.W. Dunne, the then famous author of *An Experiment with Time* in which he tried to propound a theory to explain the pre-cognitive dreams which he claimed to have had. He organized a small experiment with half a dozen of us. We wrote down our dreams every day, sent them in to our tutor and then waited to see whether any of them came true. The results were unfortunately meagre. This once impinged in a curious way on my working life. Before I was closely connected with intelligence, someone, I suppose in the CIA, had the bright idea that psychic powers could be invoked to help to provide intelligence about the activities of hostile powers. A friend knew of my interest in these subjects and I was asked to write an essay about the present state of the art in psychical research with a view to forming an opinion as to whether telepathy and clairvoyance might be used for this purpose. The conclusion was on the whole negative. Later, in retirement, I became an active member of the Society for Psychical Research and did one or two minor investigations for them of alleged cases of haunting and automatic writing.

Humanism was the end of a progressive disillusionment with established religion. I had been brought up in a conventionally religious environment. Two cousins were bishops. At school we went to chapel once a day and twice on Sundays. Doubt first arose in the course of the wide ranging 'Sunday questions' which we were asked to write on religious topics at school. I found particular difficulty, as have so many others, with the question of evil. That is to say how can an allegedly omnipotent and benign God cause or tolerate the existence of so much evil in the world? It is the question which provoked the Manichaean religions such as Zoroastrianism to invent a principle of evil separate from, and in antagonism to, the principle of good, sometimes personified as a competing deity. I won the prize for divinity at school, but this did not mean that I was endorsing the orthodox doctrines of Christianity. Later the history of the terrible things which Christians had done both to each other and to heathens completed my feeling of rejection towards Christianity and I found a much more satisfactory intellectual home in humanism. This is the view that you can build a more satisfactory system of morality and human behaviour on the basis of the proper relations of human beings to each other than by believing in the superstitions that people have erected into principles in the course of the history of religion. My course had come full circle when I rather boldly gave a lecture on humanism in the cathedral city of Chichester and was attacked (verbally!) by some of the clerics in the audience.

Reverting finally to my official life, I am quite often asked whether I would advise a young man to go into the Foreign Service now or whether it has so much changed that it is no longer a worthwhile way of life. Many things have of course changed. It is argued that two of these changes in particular have reduced the attraction of a diplomatic career. One is that with the improvement in communications, much of the work formally done by Embassies is done by peripatetic ministers and that the only useful function to be performed by Embassies is to promote British exports. I am sure it is the case that no one has time to read the long political reports which we used to write about the countries in which we were stationed, and that it is no longer necessary to have such reports because of our diminished position in the world and therefore the reduced likelihood of our being politically involved in distant countries. As regards Ministers' journeyings, however, I would suggest that they are usually too busy to know everything about the countries that they visit and that their views should be largely influenced by what the diplomats have been reporting. The other great change is that so much more of the work is done in multilateral institutions, The European Community, the United Nations, NATO, the International Monetary Fund, the World Bank etc., etc. This is not altogether a new phenomenon. How much of the history of the last two hundred years has been settled by the congresses of Vienna and Berlin, the Versailles Peace Conference, four- and then three-power government of Germany after the Second World War? The difference is that the present institutions claim to be permanent and to be dealing with the potential causes of conflict before they break out rather than after, as in the past. In any case, work in such institutions demands just as high a level of diplomatic skill as the previous conventional bilateral forms of diplomacy. This applies not only to the technical business of drawing up multilateral agreements, but also to the inter-personal skills on which old-fashioned diplomacy prided itself. People are people even in institutions.

*Ninetieth birthday party, July 3rd, 2000,
with Antonia and Rupert.*

The value of a Foreign Service career in the future has also to be judged according to how well the two elements of the process, ministers and officials, work together in trust and harmony. The political impartiality of the British Civil Service, that is to say willingness to work equally for whatever political party is in power, with freedom to argue as strongly as you like up to the point of decision, but then a wholehearted readiness to carry it out, is an asset of great value. It needs to be carefully nurtured at all times. A French colleague once told me that the French had a list of their British colleagues with their political inclinations marked against each one.

In the majority of cases I do not believe that such a list can be truthfully drawn up. I think the idea is perhaps an extrapolation of French attitudes! It is sometimes alleged that the long continuance in power of one political party tends to bend the attitudes of the civil servants in the direction of the policies of that party and therefore makes it more difficult for them to switch to another when power changes. This suggests a necessity of extra vigilance rather than the failure of the system as such. Ministers should themselves support and encourage such impartiality and they usually do. I have noted above a breakdown at the time of Suez but I think we recovered from that. One has to allow for the luck of the draw. I was lucky that I was able to feel trust and indeed admiration for the majority of the Ministers with whom I was in relatively close contact, and I think and hope that the trust was reciprocated. Of the others, perhaps the best epitaph is *De mortuis* ... if there is nothing good to be said of them, then better say nothing.

So on the whole, my answer would be 'yes', with a certain degree of hope and optimism that the best elements in the system may be maintained – or should I say restored? – and with the assurance that it is a system worth maintaining.